CAN CROCODILES CRY?

D0168541

PAUL HEINEY **CAN CROCODILES CRY?**

Amazing Answers to Mind-Blowing Questions

Illustrations: © Jenny MacKendrick, 2014

First published 2014

The History Press
The Mill, Brimscombe Port
Stroud, Gloucestershire, GL5 2QG
www.thehistorypress.co.uk

British Library Cataloguing in Publication Data.
A catalogue record for this book is available from the British Library.

ISBN 978 0 7509 6012 0

Typesetting and origination by The History Press
Printed in Great Britain

Contents

Introduction

Ask any gold miner and he'll tell you that the deeper you dig, the better the chances of finding riches. I'm beginning to feel like that gold miner, because for a few years I have been digging deep into a vast scientific archive, and it's true – the gold not only keeps appearing but it seems to get better every time I excavate. Its richness comes in the form of questions asked by thousands of young people who simply wanted to satisfy their curious minds. The answers, in return, came from a gang of dedicated scientists, all specialists in their fields, who simply wanted to give young people the satisfaction of an explanation of what was puzzling their minds.

It was inspired by a government project to encourage scientific curiosity, and it was hugely successful. It was called 'Science Line' and over a few years it was inundated with questions on everything from black holes to space travel; frogs to frostbite; cats to cataclysms. You name it, there was no subject that the enquiring minds didn't direct themselves at, and no subject the experts did not dare to tackle.

It was good fortune indeed that when the project closed the vast database of knowledge was not destroyed. Instead, like that gold miner, I have been digging deep into it to bring you, once again, some of the gems it contains.

My first harvest was called *Can Cows Walk Downstairs?*, but those 300 questions hardly skimmed the surface. Then came

Do Cats Have Belly Buttons?, and still the questions were being unearthed. Now I offer you *Can Crocodiles Cry?* to prove that there is no end to the riddles that a scientific mind can come up with.

However, in amongst the inspired, thoughtful and sometimes plain crazy questions, I did find one message from someone who was clearly having a bad day. In a moment of bad temper, he bashed out the following message: 'My Dad says that science and finding out things is a lot of fun. I don't agree.' So, how do you persuade someone that they're wrong about science? This is the reply he got, and I couldn't agree more. Read it carefully, even if you think science might not be your thing, and see if you change your mind:

> I think science is very exciting or I wouldn't spend my life doing it. I love my job and couldn't imagine doing anything different. I'm constantly finding out new things and learning about different subjects so I never get bored. However, I can remember a time when I found some bits of science boring. When I was at school for example, I found some bits of science boring because I *had* to do them and wasn't interested in them at the time. If only they'd teach me something I wanted to know.
>
> I can understand that some people might not be interested in science – that's fine. I'm not particularly interested in football, and I don't think I'd enjoy a discussion about art because I don't know much about it. Everyone's different and if you don't find science interesting, that's OK.
>
> But remember, the science you do at school isn't the only science there is.
>
> I bet you never find out why the sky is blue at school, or why your hands go wrinkly in the bath, or what shape wombat pooh is! Science is all around us and it's fascinating.

I'll go further and bet that, at school, they never taught you why clouds don't float away, why apples are round and not square, how long it takes to get to the Sun in a bus, or what makes bags under your eyes. But the answers to all those questions, and 300 more, start here …

Happy digging.

Animal Magic

Talking dogs to purring tigers;
clever cats to sleeping flies;
blinking fish to baby turtles;
yawning birds to rabbits' tails

Why can't dogs talk?

For a start, the shape of their mouths, their vocal chords and lack of a voice box are all wrong for making the sorts of sounds that humans make. We are exactly the opposite of dogs, we have long throats and small mouths and that's why we can't bark like dogs, or at least not in a way that a dog would recognise. There was once a famous dog on television in the UK who said 'sausages' – I know because I interviewed him! Have a look on YouTube – but he wasn't really saying sausages; it was the way he growled that made it sound as if he was speaking.

Talking is far more than just making sounds. The forming of words and making words into phrases and then saying them calls for a lot of brain power, and dogs simply haven't got it. Even so, dogs can 'talk' to each other in different ways and they're cleverer at it than we are. We use words to communicate, and perhaps the looks on our faces too, but dogs employ their mouths, legs and tails, bare their teeth and position their ears to get their message across. Why would they need to talk as well?

Why do dogs bark at each other?

Wouldn't it be wonderful if we really knew what dogs were trying to say to each other through their barks? What we do know is that dogs have many different types of bark – playful, nervous, excited, fearful, suspicious, stressed, even lonely. They also bark to protect their own territory and will only fight another dog if all else fails – they don't like conflict. There are many barks from 'ruff-ruff' to growling to 'yip-yip' and once you get to know your dog, you start to get a hint of what it's trying to communicate. You can be pretty certain that the first barks that two dogs exchange will be about territory – 'get off my patch!'

Why don't dogs sweat?

Sweat is the body's way of trying to control its temperature and rid itself of some unwanted chemicals. When the body is overheated, special structures in the skin send a signal to the bit of your brain that controls temperature, which then sends signals to the sweat glands to produce sweat and transport it to the surface of the skin. Evaporation of the sweat cools the skin and the body temperature drops. That's how it works for us. Animals such as dogs and cats only have sweat glands on the pads of their paws, which is not a large area. So, they have evolved to use panting as a way of controlling their temperatures by drawing cool air over their tongues. That is why you often see dogs with their tongues hanging out in hot weather. For some small animals, such as rats and mice, they cannot afford to lose water by sweating and so have no sweat glands at all.

Do dogs eat in the same way as humans?

Dogs do eat in exactly the same way as humans, contrary to appearances! The process of digestion starts when food is taken into the mouth, and is broken down both by the teeth and by saliva. The smaller particles of food then pass into the stomach where they are broken down by an assortment of chemical reactions. This is exactly the same for dogs as for humans. Dogs have larger canine teeth than we do, from having lived for a long period of their existence in the wild where they have had to hunt and kill for food with only their mouths as a weapon. They also have molars and pre-molars just as we do, and chew food to break it down, just like us. The only thing they haven't quite managed yet are table manners.

What makes cats purr and dogs bark?

Let's deal with cats first. This is a question to which there might be no proper answer, but lots of theories. One says purring is the vibration of 'false' vocal cords which are two folds of membrane behind the true cords, located in the larynx. Not all zoologists agree. Another theory suggests that purring is the direct result of turbulence in the bloodstream of the main vein returning blood to the heart from the body. This narrows in order to pass the liver and diaphragm, and the theory says that when the cat arches its back the blood forms eddies in this bottleneck. This in turn sets up vibrations in the chest which are amplified in the cavities of the skull.

It's not true that cats only purr when they're happy. Vets will tell you that cats purr while they're having all kinds of uncomfortable treatments, even when in pain. Kittens start to purr at two days old, and the mother will purr back at them, so it might be some sort of communication. Some have suggested it is a kind of self-comforting sound which a cat can make to relax itself – a cat's way of dealing with stress. It's not only domestic cats who purr. Leopards can produce deep purring sounds, as can ocelots and pumas. Cats can purr while breathing in and breathing out, and can meow at the same time.

Dogs, on the other hand, are much more communicative than cats. A dog's bark can carry far more messages than the simple purring and meowing of a cat. All this has developed over thousands of years to best suit the animal's needs. Each animal communicates with others in the best way that it can. For a dog that means barking, for a cat the purr is better.

Which are more intelligent – cats or dogs?

There's a big problem here – how can you ever work out how intelligent an animal is? For example, it's easier to train a dog to fetch a stick than it is to train a cat, but does that make the dog more intelligent, or just more obedient? The other problem is that you are not comparing like with like. It's as if you are asking 'which is more intelligent – a dolphin or an orang-utan?' They're both very clever but in completely different ways. Most animals seem to solve problems by trial and error and not by thinking about them, although it's possible that chimpanzees and some other primates do. But cats and dogs probably don't, or if they do, only to a very limited extent.

As a general rule, animals are good at things that are natural for their own species, and bad at things that their species usually doesn't do. So sheepdogs might be expected to be pretty good at problems concerned with rounding up sheep but other breeds of dog wouldn't. And of course cats would be hopeless – they're just not built for it! Which doesn't answer the question, to which there is no real answer.

Why do cats sniff each other's noses when they first meet?

They're just being polite. In other words, it's their way of saying, 'Hello, how are you, where have you come from?' It is cat communication. We shake hands, they rub noses. It's possible they do it because of something in the saliva or on the breath that makes each cat unique. From this they can tell sex, maturity and possibly social status. So a good sniff is as good as a biography. Also remember that a cat's close-up eyesight is not very good and so they have to rely on other signals to recognise other cats. But they don't just rub noses. They sometimes sniff each other's bottoms to get the same information. Incidentally, if your cat turns away and shows you its bottom, don't be insulted – it's simply trying to tell that at that particular moment you are the number one person in its life.

Why do cats have two eyelids?

They don't – they have three. There's a top and bottom eyelid, just like us, and then the third one. Dogs and rabbits also have them. It's called a nictitating membrane. The eyelid has a tear gland on one side that helps keep the eye moist. This is the most important function of the eyelid, as the tears contain antibodies that help deal with infection. When cats fight they have a special mechanism that pulls the eye back a little way into its socket, and this allow the third eyelid to appear and provide added protection. If you want to see a cat's third eyelid, look for it after your cat has just woken up from a long, deep sleep.

Can a tiger purr like my cat?

About 100 years ago an experiment was done in which scientists divided cats (large and small) into two groups depending on how bones and muscles at the base of their tongues were arranged. In one group of cats, the tongue and larynx were only loosely connected to the skull. In this group were tigers, lions, jaguars, leopards and snow leopards. These cats cannot purr, but they can roar. In the other group, which included the mountain lion and domestic cats, the arrangement of bones was slightly different and these cats can purr, but they cannot roar. Incidentally, the cats in the first group have round pupils in their eyes, and in the second the pupil is mostly a vertical slit.

My tabby cat has some hairs with different colours along their length. Why is this?

The colours in a cat's fur are due to the presence of a pigment called melanin in the hairs. Melanin is usually black, although it can be converted to a chocolate brown colour. Sometimes, the hairs do not contain any pigment and then they are white. All cat coat patterns are made up of different combinations of these and other colours.

The pattern and colour of any cat's coat depends on which colour pigment is produced and when, and this is controlled by the cat's genes. In some cats, the hairs are the same colour along their entire length, but in other cats the colour of the hairs varies along the length. Sometimes the hair is yellow/brown for most of its length but with a black tip, or sometimes the hair has black bands all the way along it. This happens because the melanocytes (the cells which produce the pigments) produce different kinds of melanin at different stages in the hair's growth.

Most mammals you see in the wild, such as brown rabbits or mice, have a flecked appearance which is good for camouflage.

My cat's got fleas. My dog's got fleas. Are they the same flea?

Bad luck. Cat fleas and dog fleas are actually different types of fleas. If you want to give them names they are *Ctenocephalides felis* and *Ctenocephalides canis*. However, there aren't many fleas which only live on dogs; but there are far more cat fleas because cat fleas will quite happily live on any host they can find – which could be anything from a dog to a human being. Most fleas will feed and breed on a variety of hosts. An example of this is the cat flea which infects not only the domestic cat but dogs,

foxes, mongooses, opossums, leopards, and other mammals, including man if nothing else is around.

Monkeys and apes do not get fleas, nor do horses. But fleas love rats, mice and squirrels because they tend to build their nests in holes which provide the right conditions for fleas to breed. Fleas feed on blood, but can survive for a long time without food. The rabbit flea, for example, can live for nine months at temperatures around the freezing point without feeding.

Can tarantulas change sex?

When tarantulas are young they all look like females, but as they get older their sex becomes more obvious. Adult males have hooks on their front legs and their stomachs, and are smaller than females. The males' 'pedipalps' (the feely bits that stick out of the head) are shaped like clubs. It may take ten moults – seven years – for these differences to become obvious. So, it might look as though tarantulas change sex when they moult; but they don't, it's just that the differences between males and females become more obvious.

How far can ants see?

Some worker ants have well-developed eyes and can leap from branch to branch. Some have tiny eyes, and worker army ants, which are the most aggressive ants in the world, will eat anything that gets in their way even though they are blind. They use their antennae for smell and touch but they have no eyes at all. However, the jumping ants of India, unlike most ants, can jump to catch prey and have two large eyes to help them navigate. But the picture their eyes provide is not like the one we would see. Ants' eyes are 'compounded' so, instead of seeing one big picture, it would be more like looking at a shop window full of television sets all showing the same picture.

How strong is an ant?

Ants can carry up to fifty times their own body weight on their back, and their pincers can grip something 1,400 times their weight. The reason they can lift things many times their body weight is all down to simple physics. Their muscles are no stronger than human muscles but, because they have a very small body mass the proportion of their mass that is muscle is very high. With elephants it's the reverse – the proportion of their mass that is muscle is low so they can't lift their own body weight. If we were as small as ants, we'd be able to lift weights like they do.

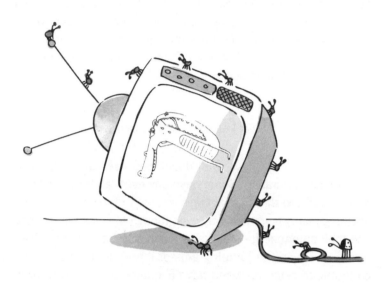

By the way, some ants can be pretty aggressive. Army ants are called 'swarm feeders' and hunt just like an army. They eat lizards, snakes, goats, scorpions and beetles, and an army of them can consume 100,000 creatures a day!

Why don't flies knock themselves out when they fly into windows?

Basically, houseflies don't have enough momentum to stun themselves. If they flew faster they might – we all know what happens to a fly when it hits the windscreen of a car travelling at speed. Or if they were heavier they might – some heavier beetles like cockchafers and stag beetles can stun themselves by flying into windows.

Where do flies go in winter?

Flies, like all other insects, are cold-blooded so they can't regulate their temperature internally. When warm-blooded creatures, such as ourselves, get cold we can warm ourselves up to some extent by shivering. When cold-blooded creatures get cold they can't warm themselves up so they can't actually do much about it. Insects, including flies, can cope with the cold winter in three different ways. They can try and muddle through as best they can, and this is what some of the smaller species of fly do. Others hibernate, and emerge in the spring when the weather gets warmer. However, the vast majority of flies lay eggs and then die. The eggs sit quietly in a corner until the spring when they hatch and produce a new generation of flies.

Where does the bluebottle fly sleep at night?

Like most insects they don't go to sleep in the sense that we do, but they do take a rest. Their breathing and heart rate slows and so they use less energy. They don't close their eyes like we do, because they don't have eyelids. Even though they are resting they still have to remain on alert because predators are everywhere, waiting to pounce. As far as bluebottles are concerned, like flies, they don't sleep but simply take a pause from buzzing around and start again as soon as the sun comes up.

Why do flies whizz around the light bulb, even when the light is off?

No one's really sure why they fly around the light bulb. Some say it's because it's the middle of the room and flies don't like corners. Another theory says they tend to stay in the middle of the room searching for a perch as it is the best position to fight off a rival or for attracting a mate. Male flies tend to establish a 'lek-type mating assembly' around ceiling lights – that's when they get together and display themselves to attract females. Female houseflies that are aiming to perch on the light fitting are intercepted by any male lucky enough to be patrolling the airspace closest by. Males therefore compete to occupy the top position, and will chase out any other flies which are threatening to invade their airspace. The next time that you see a housefly circling purposefully beneath one of your ceiling lights, try throwing a fake fly at it – a bit of fly-sized paper will do. The fly will almost certainly break from its horizontal circling to chase the 'intruder' away.

Why do snails only come out at night?

Actually, they will come out at any time of day, it's just that they prefer the darkness. Snails have a moist surface to their bodies which allows water to pass inwards or outwards very easily. If they spent too long in the sunshine it is quite likely they could become dehydrated by evaporation, so they aren't out and about as much in broad daylight.

How many eyes does an earthworm have?

The simple answer to this is that they have none. Earthworms are very basic creatures. They have no eyes or ears. However, their entire body, particularly the upper surface, is incredibly sensitive, especially to light. They can also sense vibration and will easily detect the movement of a mole – earthworms will quickly rise to the surface if they sense one is digging close to them. However, they won't stay on the surface long, because if exposed to too much light they become paralysed. What makes them so sensitive is that they have a nervous system which runs the entire length of their body. They don't have brains, but they do have a large collection of nerves which bundle together in the head region of a worm.

Did you know that in one acre of land there can be as many as a million worms?

If you cut a worm in half, will it live?

It will depend where the cut is, and which bit of the worm you're talking about. The bit with the head in it might well survive and it could attempt to grow a new tail, but the bit without a head would certainly die. In order to repair itself, the front part of the worm must contain the clitellum – a kind of gland which looks a bit like a saddle – and about ten segments after that. Any shorter and your worm will die. Not all worms can perform this trick, so it would also depend on which type of worm you are talking about.

Can fish see in the dark?

A fish eye has a very large pupil which allows a lot of light into the eye, so fish can see in much darker conditions than we can. But to be able to see there has to be *some* light. Some fish live very deep down in the dark ocean in what we call the 'twilight zone', and at these depths they can employ organs called photophores which give off light and can be arranged in lines or patterns across the fish's body. They can use these photophores as a sort of searchlight, or for dazzling other fish and attracting food.

Do fish blink?

No, they don't have moveable eyelids but they do have one transparent eye protector over their eyes all the time. They don't have a problem with keeping eye tissues moist – there's plenty of moisture around – but like all eyes they need protecting from sharp objects and dirt. Fish eyes are actually quite amazing. They have excellent eyesight and can see parts of the spectrum we can't, like UV (ultraviolet). Some can also distinguish polarised light, which can improve contrast so that other fish might become more visible.

How do you measure the memory of goldfish?

One way of testing the memory of a goldfish is with an underwater maze which has food at the end. Once the goldfish has learned its way through the maze you can wait and see how long it takes for the fish to forget. An alternative is a test where fish are presented with two boxes, only one of which has food in. The fish can be trained to learn which of the boxes contains the food and, again, you can wait to see how long the fish remembers this. There's a myth that goldfish only have a three-second memory – some scientists say it's as long as twenty-four hours, others think it might be as long as five months.

Do fish have hearts?

Fish do have a heart but it only has two chambers, unlike our heart which has four. This is because the fish heart only pumps blood around the body, whereas our heart has to pump blood around the body and also around the lungs. Fish don't have lungs because they get oxygen from the water around them, using their gills. In a fish, the blood enters the heart through a vein and exits through a vein on its way to the gills. In the gills, the blood picks up oxygen from the surrounding water and leaves the gills in arteries, which go to the rest of the body. The oxygen is used in the body and the blood goes back to the heart.

Why do fish have scales?

Scales are small overlapping bony plates which provide greater protection for the fish. They are a kind of exoskeleton, like the shell of a crab. It's like body armour.

Do fish sweat?

Mammals which live surrounded by air, cool themselves by evaporating moisture from their skin. Fish have no such means of maintaining a constant body temperature, and their blood is usually at the same temperature as their surroundings, which is the water they're in. So, fish have no need to sweat. Most fish will die if the water becomes too hot or too cold, or changes temperature too suddenly. This is why care is needed when transferring fish into a new aquarium so that they have sufficient time to adapt to the temperature of their new surroundings.

Can fish love each other?

I suppose you're asking if fish have emotions. It's impossible for us to tell how a fish feels about anything, but there was once an interesting experiment: a female fish, ready to mate, was put in a tank with two males. She formed an association with one of them. Let's call it love. The two males then started to fight

over her and scientists studied her brain responses while she watched them. Certain parts of her brain became highly active at moments when her boyfriend was taking a beating. What does that tell you? It certainly doesn't prove love between them; you can't simply translate brain activity into feelings. But that experiment comes under the heading of 'very interesting'...

Why don't whales get the bends?

Let's be clear about what 'the bends' are. When people dive deep into the sea they wear a diving tank and are breathing air at higher pressures than normal, which means pressure is built up in the body. If they change their external pressure too quickly, by suddenly rising to the surface for example, then the absorbed gas is released too quickly in the form of bubbles throughout the body. It's also called 'compression sickness' and gives rise to painful joints, paralysis and possible death – that's in humans.

Whales, however, take a breath while on the surface and before they dive, and don't breathe again while they're underwater, so they're not taking in any pressurised air. In fact, whales can breathe out as they dive and collapse their lungs in order to fill their blood with as much oxygen as possible. That's why the bends is not a problem for them.

Is whale poo huge?

Whale faeces (or 'poo' to you and me) will contain undigested materials like fish eyes and squid beaks, depending on what the whale's been eating. Whales are mammals and, just like any other mammals, their digestive system will produce waste organic materials. It is difficult to describe exactly what form this takes because it's shed directly into the sea and breaks down, but generally speaking it will tend to be in liquid form. Sometimes, though, it can float for a while and then sink while dissolving in the water.

Why can't whales move when they are beached?

Whales swim by moving their tails, or 'flukes' as they are more accurately known. Upthrust is important for anything floating in water. Unless you have an upthrust equal to the force downwards, you will not float. Upthrust is created by displacement. As you push the water out of the way, the water pushes back and this is what makes you float. As whales are so large, when they beach their bodies can't support themselves without the help of the upthrust and so they become helpless.

How do turtles breathe underwater?

Turtles don't always need to breathe underwater. Sea turtles can hold their breath for up to five hours, and could spend that long submerged. They're also cold-blooded creatures and have a slow metabolism so don't have the same urgent need for oxygen as we do. If they're swimming hard they may come up and take a breath much more often; if they're resting then they can hold their breath for hours.

How do baby turtles find their way to the sea?

Their mothers don't help them, because once they have laid their eggs they return to the sea, so the newborn turtles follow the daylight instead. The sea is usually brighter than the land, and even at night it reflects some light, so the little turtles use that to guide them. In fact, they prefer to make the journey at night because it makes it more difficult for predators to spot them. Even more remarkable is the fact that once they have found the ocean, they can then swim for 5,000 miles and still find their way home. No one knows how they do it. It's such a risky thing, being a baby turtle, that only one in a thousand will survive to become fully grown.

How long do sharks live?

The great white shark becomes mature when it reaches 11–14ft, and by the age of 14 it will reach 16ft. After this, they can reach ages of up to 40 years, although some say it could be as much as 100 years. Smaller sharks might live for twenty to forty years. The truth is we know very little about the lifespan of sharks.

Can male seahorses have babies?

Yes, they can. What happens is that the females lay their eggs in their partners' pouches, so it is the males that eventually carry the offspring. They do this for three weeks, and go through about seventy-two hours of labour before the baby seahorses emerge – there might be as many as 200 of them. A lot of people think that seahorses only exist in stories, but they are real enough. They may have evolved at least 40 million years ago, and have changed very little since.

Is it true that a bird eats bits out of alligators' teeth?

It might be a bit of a tall story, but there again it might just be true. The Egyptian plover and the spur-winged plover are most likely to be the brave ones who perform this trick, because they both feed close to basking crocodiles. The common sandpiper also feeds near crocodiles in Africa during the northern winter. All three of these bird species are 'waders', or shorebirds, and are very brave!

How strong is a crocodile's bite?

The muscles that close a crocodile's jaws are very strong. They crush turtle shells with ease, and a large saltwater crocodile holding a pig's head can simply crush the skull by flexing the muscles from a standing start. But the muscles involved in opening the jaws have little strength. A rubber band around the snout is enough to prevent a 2m-long crocodile from opening its mouth.

Can Crocodiles Cry?

Have you heard an expression called 'crying crocodile tears'? It means when someone cries but the sadness is not genuine. For example, the school rings up and says the exams have been cancelled and you burst into tears. In fact, you're over the moon, but you want everyone to think you're disappointed. Those are called 'crocodile tears'.

There's a difference between producing tears, which is a physical response, and real crying, which is an emotional response. In the case of crocodiles, they can produce tears from lachrymal glands pretty similar to our own, and these tears are used to lubricate the front of the eye. Crocodiles don't cry because they're sad, like we do, although the legend goes that crocodiles produce tears in order to lure prey. It's a myth, and it goes all the way back to the thirteenth century when a monk wrote, 'If the crocodile findeth a man by the brim of the water … he slayeth him there if he may, and then weepeth upon him.' If you were to watch a crocodile closely while it was eating its prey, it might look as if it were crying. This may be because the huge force that comes into play when a crocodile bites down hard, squeezes the tear ducts and creates a weeping effect.

Why has the crocodile survived, but the dinosaur didn't?

For a start, dinosaurs and crocodiles came from very distinct groups. Crocodiles are animals that are very flexible in their response to environmental change, whereas dinosaurs evidently weren't. You might as well ask why turtles, snakes and lizards survived when the dinosaurs died out; the explanation is the same. These animals were able to adapt to changes in their environment. Whether this involved them becoming scavengers, or lowering their metabolic rate, or living in a hole in the ground doesn't really matter; the fact remains they were able to do this. The dinosaurs simply weren't smart enough.

Do any animals cry?

Tricky one to answer – opinions are divided on this. Chimps certainly do get upset, but whether they cry to express their unease is not certain. Perhaps the moisture is simply the natural product of the eye. You've got to separate crying as a way of an animal cleansing its eyes, and crying to express an emotion, like sadness. No one is quite sure if sadness is something that animals experience, or whether it is only found in humans. It is believed by some that elephants can produce tears from emotion, but until we have a way of understanding what animals really feel, how can we know?

If squid are colour blind, why do they colour change to communicate?

It's true that squid are colour blind, but they work round it by observing patterns rather than the colours themselves. On a squid's skin, you'll find cells of many different colours, and these can be made to expand or contract. All the squid has to do is decide the colour it wants to be and send the appropriate signals to the nerves that control what are called the 'chromatophores'. These cells, which allow a creature to change its colour, are also found in frogs, chameleons and cuttlefish. Interesting fact – the eye of a squid is remarkably similar to a human eye, even though we are not related.

If cows only eat grass, where does the milk come from?

For a start, cows need a lot of food. They might eat well over 50lb of grass a day as well as drink 50 gallons of water. From the grass the cow gets protein, energy, vitamins and minerals – all of which are the building blocks of milk (and muscle). All of those ingredients are converted into milk by a very complicated chemical process, but before you get any milk the cow has to have given birth, and it is the sucking of the calf on the cow's udder that starts the flow of milk. As long as the cow is milked either by a calf or by a machine, she will keep producing. Once she stops being milked, her udder will slowly dry up till she has another calf. Making milk is hard work. It can take a cow up to seventy hours to turn grass into milk and, for every litre she makes, 400 litres of blood must pass through her udder.

Is there an animal that can be broken into bits to make new individuals?

Yes, providing it's not into too many bits. Starfish can grow new arms if they lose one and can even regrow themselves completely from just one arm, providing there's still a little bit of the central disc attached. It takes about a year for a new starfish to grow. Incidentally, they are not fish. They don't have gills, scales or fins, and move around by using tiny tubes on their arms. They've also got an eye, although it's pretty crude and isn't much more than a red spot at the end of each arm, but it can tell light from dark.

Starfish have funny eating habits too. To eat a mussel inside its shell, first they will grab the mussel with their arms, open the shell a little, then they will push their own stomach up through their mouths and into the shell. They then wrap the stomach round the mussel and devour it. Clever, eh? It's a way of making them able to feed on things which are much bigger than their tiny mouths. The starfish is thought to be the only creature which does this.

Do bees talk to each other?

They tell each other where flowers are to be found so they can collect the nectar, and they do this by dancing. The style of the dance tells the other bees how far away the food is. There's a 'round' dance, which says the food is close by. Then there's the much more complicated 'waggle' dance which is usually done in the privacy of the hive. Although the other bees might not see it they can feel it, and the dancer emits little piping noises so they can hear it as well. The waggle dance is in the shape of a figure of eight with a line down the middle and the direction of the straight line is a pointer to where the food is to be found. This theory was first put forward by scientist Karl von Frisch, who was awarded the Nobel prize in 1973.

When a bee stings does it die?

Once a honey bee has stung you, yes it will die. But not all species of bees do, and it is only female bees and wasps that can sting. In the case of bumblebees, their stings have tiny barbs, but these can be easily retracted once the bee has given you a sting. It can happen so quickly that the bee will be on its way again before you feel the pain. But, with honey bees, the barbs are much larger and in order to fly off, the bee has to force its entire stinging apparatus away from its body. This is what kills it.

How do bees navigate?

They use the sun, pretty much as we would if we had no compass. It is thought that bees remember where things are in relation to the Sun at the time they found them. To that they add information which comes from their internal clock which tells

them, in effect, how far they have flown. But it's cleverer than that, because bees also use the time to work out how far the Sun has moved while they have been in flight, and can pass onto the other bees in the hive the position of the food in relation to the Sun as it is now, and not as it was when they found it. Then they do a little dance (see above) and the message spreads through the hive. As part of the growing-up process, a young bee will learn how the sun's path across the sky changes with the seasons and can add that to the other information to give precise navigation. Bees don't often get lost.

What are wasps for?

I hate wasps and you probably do too, especially when they spoil a picnic on a summer's afternoon. But wasps are quite an important part of the insect food chain. For a start they will eat many pests which might otherwise do damage to crops, such as caterpillars. They will also control whitefly in greenhouses. They also feed on nectar and so can help in pollination, and there would be far more flies in the world if it wasn't for wasps.

Do wasps find their way around in the same way as bees?

Bees have evolved from wasps which means that bees might be a bit cleverer at navigation. It seems that wasps can't communicate as well as bees, and they can be easily confused. Wasps recognise their home by circling the nest and recognising the landscape. If you then either move the nest or change the landscape, the wasp will return to the same spot even if the nest has been moved. It's as if you always returned to the same tree outside your house, even if someone moved the house.

Does anything eat bees?

For a start, your dog might have a go, as many dogs do, but they soon discover the mistake they've made. Cats will have a go too. But certainly crab spiders will eat bees – crab spiders don't make webs, but hang around flowers waiting to pounce – and badgers and skunks will raid a bee nest. Some birds – tits and shrikes amongst them – have cleverly learnt to remove the sting before trying to eat them. Foxes will eat bees, and bears will eat them too – which is stupid of them because they'd be far happier if they ate the honey instead.

Why doesn't the blood in bats run to their heads when they're hanging upside down?

Bat hearts are large relative to their body size and they also have high stroke volumes, which means they pump a lot of blood with every heartbeat. In addition there are anti-backflow

valves in the heart, and in the arteries, veins, and capillaries in the flight membranes. So the combination of large hearts, high heart rates, and high stroke volumes assists their upside-down resting position.

What do humans look like to animals, and what do other animals look like?

First of all, animals see things differently to the way we see things, and different types of animals have different kinds of sight. For example, eagles have incredibly good long vision and cats are incredibly sensitive to differences in light and dark, which is what makes them good hunters.

As far as recognising their own species, animals rely on smell rather than sight. New-born mammals are licked clean by their mother at birth, which allows the mother to imprint the smell of their offspring. At the same time, the baby learns the scent of its mother and this allows them to recognise each other. So mammals very much rely on scent recognition. Birds do have a sense of smell, but rely more on visual patterns. The pattern of wing feathers, or the song of a particular bird, will identify one bird to another. As far as mammals go, a cow will look like a cow to another cow, but much more important is the scent of an animal which conveys a lot more information than sight alone.

Animals may well see humans as 'two-legs' or whatever, but what is far more important is our scent. If you were to show a dog a photograph of its owner, or even a life-sized cardboard cut-out, it wouldn't recognise them. But it would be able to recognise one of her shirts, or a favourite chair he sits in.

Can animals see colours?

Most mammals appear to be colour-blind, although some primates and a few other species such as squirrels, and perhaps cats, can detect colours. Birds, lizards, turtles, frogs and bony fishes all have colour vision. In fact, a bird's colour vision is probably better than that of primates. Cats have a certain amount of colour vision, but it is not as good as ours. They appear to see blue and green but not very much red, and even then the colours are very wishy-washy, a bit like we would see at dawn or dusk. However, cats are hunters and their eyes are therefore far better adapted to low-light vision than ours.

Red/green colour-blindness is common in humans, and dogs too. They only have two of the three types of 'cones' – the colour-sensing cells found in the retina at the back of the eye. This makes it difficult for them to detect red, which might appear to them as muddy brown or possibly black. If you're buying a dog blanket, red might not be the best colour to choose.

Crocodiles can see in colour and have sophisticated eyes which make them very sensitive to low light levels. This is essential as crocodiles are active by night as well as by day. They also have colour-sensing cone cells in their eyes, and it's thought they may be sensitive to polarised light which would enable them to spot prey through the reflections off the surface of water.

And penguins can see in colour too.

Why are birds' eggs coloured?

It's to camouflage them and protect them from predators, especially for those birds which lay their eggs on the ground. The colouring happens like this: after the egg has been formed inside the bird, it passes down a long tube called the oviduct. It is here that the egg can be coated with pigments. If the egg is stationary in the oviduct then it will be spotted; if it is moving when the colour is applied it will be streaky. Although birds' eggs may be anything from blue to red to green, the colouring is produced by just two pigments, one of which can result in eggshell colours of pale yellow all the way up to black, and is related to the bird's haemoglobin. The other pigment is a bluish green pigment that comes from bile.

Why do birds ruffle their feathers?

It's exactly the same as when we pull a coat collar up around our necks. By ruffling their feathers, birds create a small pocket of air between the surface of their skin and their feathers and it helps to keep them warm.

Do birds yawn?

Yes they do, but that's about all we know about bird yawning – or any other kind of yawning for that matter. It's all very mysterious. In humans we have thought that it might be to get a rush of oxygen to our brains to help us keep awake, or to get us ready for sleep. But these are all really guesses.

Yawning is very catching. If one person in a rooms yawns then others will soon follow. I'm yawning now, simply writing this. Some social animals, such as parrots, will also join in and chickens often yawn when they wake in the morning. One theory says that in birds it's a way of controlling body temperature – it has been observed that birds yawn more often in warmer weather.

Can birds taste things?

Birds do have taste buds on the back of the tongue but many fewer than in mammals. Quail, chicken, pigeon and finches might have around fifty, compared with 10,000 in humans. Even with only a few taste buds birds can taste and smell, but it is unclear how well they can discriminate between different tastes.

The birds have stopped singing. Why?

Is it summer where you are? If so, that's the reason. One of the main reasons for birdsong is to mark territory, which is very important during the breeding season. But once that season is over (usually at the end of spring or into summer) the majority of birds will keep quiet. So it's normal behaviour. An exception is the robin, which sings all year round.

Why do smaller birds sing sweeter songs?

There's no real relationship between size and song-making ability. House sparrows are practically tone deaf, while the larger blackbird and song thrush have intricate patterns of song. The robin is closely related to the sweet-sounding nightingale; finches are not very good generally, but chaffinches are considered to have a good song. Most thrushes tend to be good singers, with the one exception being the field fare which has the most limited repertoire. Starlings have the greatest repertoire, and the best ability to copy and mimic. Size doesn't really have much to do with it, but it's true that a skylark is much more musical than a fat, old crow.

Why do magpies like shiny things?

Magpies like any sort of small object that they might be able to use to build their nest, shiny or not. Other birds like organic bits and pieces for nest-building, like twigs and leaves, but magpies will build their nests out of anything they can find or steal. A magpie's nest is usually a very messy one. The reason why people may think that magpies like shiny things is because it is much easier to see a shiny thing in a magpie's mouth as it is flying past than it is to see something dull. Magpies are very curious birds and like playing with all sorts of things. This is especially true of tame or captive magpies. There's also a theory that magpies use shiny objects in order to attract a mate.

Why don't you see any birds in trees at night?

They are there, but they might be hiding. Birds do sleep in trees at night but they roost in dense areas and under leaves and branches in order to keep out of the wind and rain, and to hide from predators. So they are there, you just don't see them.

Why don't birds fall off the branches when they go to sleep?

They've got a tendon on the back of their ankle which flexes and locks their feet into position round the branch. As soon as they wake up and want to fly off, the tendon relaxes and away they go.

What sort of trail would a millipede leave?

Millipede means 'thousand legs'. You'd need to put it on something like talcum powder to see it, as its 'footprints' are very light. Millipedes can have any number of legs. A young one might have twenty, an older millipede could have hundreds, especially if it is the large kind found in hot places like Africa. The legs move in waves along each side, so you would be likely to see a cluster of closely spaced small dots, and then another and then another. They move in straight lines, so the dots would be in straight lines.

Do lizards have snot?

Let's call it mucus, and lizards certainly have mucus. They have large areas of mucus-producing membranes in their mouths and they use it as a kind of weapon to capture ants before they eat them. In some lizards, the mucus is poisonous to other creatures and is part of the lizard's way of capturing food.

How old are cockroaches?

It's thought they may have been around for at least 280 million years, so they deserve some respect. However, most people consider them a pest. They like warmth and water, and if there's some food as well they will thrive. That's why they like kitchens a lot. They are remarkable creatures. They bleed white blood, their skeleton is on the outside of their body, and as they grow they shed their external skeleton several times a year. A cockroach that has shed its skin is white with black eyes. After eight hours it will regain its regular shell colouring. A cockroach can live for a week without its head. The roach only dies because without a mouth it can't drink water and dies of thirst. They can hold their breath for forty minutes. I suppose all that makes them pretty indestructible, which may be why they've lasted so long.

Why do some spiders build vertical webs and others build horizontal ones?

Vertical webs catch flying insects, while horizontal webs, such as sheet webs, catch crawling and jumping insects, so it all comes down to what the spider would normally prey on.

Do chickens have teeth?

Chickens do not have teeth, not nowadays, and it is thought they lost them about 80 million years ago. They don't need them now because a tough beak and a hard tongue is plenty strong enough for the food they eat, such as grains. Have you heard the expression 'as rare as hen's teeth'? Now you know where it comes from.

When a butterfly sees a caterpillar, does it think 'that used to be me'?

It's extremely unlikely because they're just not clever enough. Butterflies don't have any higher-order consciousness, and so have no sense of time or self, both of which you would need to recognise caterpillars as being a former life. Butterflies probably don't even recognise other butterflies. All they need to know is that they're the same species, of the opposite sex, and ready to mate.

Are moles blind?

No they're not. It's true that moles have very tiny eyes, but that doesn't matter because they're spending most of their time underground anyway. Perhaps you're thinking of a species called the blind mole rat, found in the Middle East and parts of Africa, which has very degenerated, sunken eyes, completely grown over with skin. They haven't got any ears either. These moles are totally blind, and the brain structures responsible for imaging are also shrunken or absent. However, they can detect light through a photo-pigment which turns light into nerve signals. This is a very unusual situation for an animal that's blind, and it's the first time it has been found in a blind, burrowing mammal.

One other remarkable thing – blind mole rats can't get cancer due to a unique mechanism in which the cancerous cells produce a poisonous protein which kills the cancer cells. Needless to say, this makes these creatures very interesting to scientists who are trying to understand how cancer works.

Where do ants go in the winter?

Ants live in colonies in huge nests with hundreds and hundreds of them. Each ant has got a job. There are workers, soldiers, nurses looking after grubs, and of course the queen who does nothing but lay eggs. The queen of a colony can live up to twenty years. The others don't live quite so long. During the summer and autumn you may see lots of ants scurrying around looking for food, but when the weather starts to get cold the entrance to the colony is sealed up and the ants go deep inside. Here they partially hibernate, doing only what is required to keep things ticking over. Over winter, they survive because they have built up food stores in their body which they can use to get through the winter until the weather improves. When spring comes, the entrance to the colony gets unplugged, and the ants start being busy workers again!

Do ants have blood?

Ants do have blood, but it will not be the same as human blood because they don't rely on blood to carry oxygen around their bodies as we do. Ants have no blood vessels, the blood simply fills in the spaces between their organs.

Where do moths go during the day?

Since moths love light bulbs, you'd think they'd love the daylight as well. The reason they don't is because it's not safe – there are more predators around in the daytime. It is often the case that a lot of creature behaviour can be put down to avoiding their enemies.

How moths find their way around in the dark is interesting. They use the Moon as a steady reference point and fly in a straight line-keeping the Moon on one side. When a bright artificial light is present, like a candle flame, they try to do the same thing and that's why they end up flying round in circles. The brightness of the light disorientates them and their orbits get smaller and smaller until eventually they hit the light. To communicate in the dark, moth species emit a smelly hormone which other moths can detect from distances of several kilometres.

When do clothes moths lay their eggs?

Moths have a very strange diet. They love a mixture of the fur and wool of an animal, plus a certain amount of fungal material. You can often find plenty on clothes made from natural materials. They have developed an almost unique ability to digest keratin, which is the protein that makes up fur, wool, hair and feathers, toenails and dead skin. All that makes for a perfect moth meal. The female moth lays 50–100 eggs over a period of two to three weeks and dies after laying. The laying period is towards the autumn. The eggs are attached to fabric with an adhesive and hatch in about a week in very warm conditions. How fast the larvae grow depends on the quality of the food. On raw wool or rabbit fur they may become moths in three or four months. On average, it takes from four to six months for an egg to turn into a moth, but an adult moth may only live for two to three weeks.

Why do elephants only live in Africa and India?

Elephants and mammoths once lived all over the world, and fossils have been found just about everywhere except Australia and Antarctica. Elephant remains have even been found in England, but because the Australian and Antarctic continents have always been islands, the elephants never made it there. However, elephants can be very good swimmers and their vast bodies mean they can float easily, and by using all four legs they can get up quite a speed. There have been reports of elephants swimming for up to six hours without touching the bottom. In Europe, elephant-like creatures were possibly wiped out by a wave of extinctions, as climate conditions changed. They may also have been hunted to extinction by early humans.

Can monkeys swim?

Most monkeys hate water and avoid it, which is why they can't escape from an island even if the surrounding water is shallow.

They just don't like the stuff. Some monkeys *will* swim, though. The rule seems to be that the smaller the monkey, the more it seems to like the water. The big ones, like the apes, gorillas and chimps, hate getting into their swimming trunks.

Why are flamingos pink?

It's because of what they eat. Flamingos are born with grey feathers which gradually turn pink as they grow. The colour comes from carotene, which is a chemical pigment in the microscopic shrimps, prawns and plankton which the birds feed on. Some zoos make up food from vegetables such as carrots which contain that pigment, just to make sure the flamingos stay that colour.

And why do they stand on one leg?

They sleep on one leg to stop their feet from becoming too cold, so they lift one foot out of the cold water and swap feet every so often.

Why have rabbits got white tails?

It's really the underside of their tail that's white. It's a warning signal to other rabbits. When a rabbit sees the white flash of another's tail, it knows it's time to run. However, a German scientist has another idea – he thinks that the white flash on the tail is to attract predators, who focus on the white spot while they chase. When the rabbit makes a sharp turn, as rabbits can, the spot disappears and the predator becomes confused so the rabbit gets away.

Where do ducks have their ears?

Same place as you and me – on the sides of their heads. But they don't stick out. Instead, the opening of the ear canal is covered with a layer of special protective feathers which stop the water getting in. That's why we can't see them. Apparently, ducks have very good hearing – almost as good as ours.

Why do wolves howl at the Moon?

It's not the Moon they're howling at; it's just that when we hear it it's usually during the night when the Moon is out. The howl of a wolf can do two things – it can call a pack together, or it can warn of danger and signal others to keep away. The reason the other wolves in the pack join in is simply so they can be part of the conversation.

How high does a grasshopper jump?

A grasshopper can typically perform a long jump of about 1m, or a high jump of 0.5m. Jump distance and/or height are proportional to the amount of energy that can be delivered to the legs during take-off. But how does a grasshopper manage to develop such a large force in such a short space of time? The answer is in the anatomy of their legs – they're using them as a form of catapult. On the back legs of a grasshopper are a pair of springs, made from a special cuticle (which is like stuff that insect skeletons are made of). This cuticle is very stiff and can store a lot of energy, rather like the strong elastic in a catapult. This incredible mechanism can generate a final take-off velocity of roughly 7mph, with an acceleration of about 20g. A fighter pilot would black out at g-forces far lower than this.

Why do most animals walk on four legs?

Most animals walk on four legs as it provides a larger area of support, enabling them to balance better. These animals have bone and muscle structures developed especially for their movement. Primates move on all fours, using their hind limbs to do most of the work. Humans have evolved from primates and have therefore inherited the ability of walking on two limbs from primates too. However, humans are the only mammal able to walk or run on two legs.

Is there a reason why mammals with four legs run faster than ones with two legs?

There's no single reason, but it may be to do with balance. Four-legged animals are naturally balanced, with their centre of gravity falling under the body and within the area formed by the three or four supporting legs. Humans are different in that the centre of gravity falls into a relatively small area between the feet when they're standing still, but falls outside that area when they're moving. A lot more muscular energy in the back and buttocks has to be used to keep the body from falling forward. In four-legged animals, this power and energy can be used to move the animal forward. Some four-legged animals are also able to use their spines to increase gait and thus speed – think of cheetahs or greyhounds. Humans cannot do this.

Another factor is that humans waste energy and power with vertical body movements; for example, your head tends to bob up and down as you walk. Some two-legged movers have overcome some of the problems – a kangaroo can go pretty fast, but it wastes energy and power in the vertical component of the hop, so the swinging tail helps instead to catapult the animal along. Humans might be better off with a tail.

The Human Body

Forgetting things
to bionic eyes;
taste buds to teeth;
popping ears to smelly wee;
floating fat to phantom pain

When you forget something, where has the memory gone?

Firstly, a word about memory. The reason people exist at all is because of two important things – memory and language. Our ancestors needed language to explain how to light a fire to keep their caves warm, and a memory to remember how to do it. So really, we have a memory because if we didn't we would never have evolved far enough for you to ask this question in the first place.

It's a mistake to think that human memory works like computer memory – it's far more complicated than that. For a start, it doesn't all live in the same part of the brain, because we need to remember so much information that our brains simply wouldn't be big enough. So, we have 'short term' memory and the brain picks out the most important things in that and then shifts them to 'long term' memory. Short term memory really is short, and that's why you might find it easy to remember an eight-digit phone number, but when it gets above twelve digits it becomes more difficult. So, when you forget something it may be because it has moved from your short term into your long term memory. It will be in there somewhere, if only you can find it. Of course, it's possible that in moving from one memory to the other it might have got 'scrambled' or be incomplete, in which case you'll never find it. As an example, you might think you remember the coat you were wearing yesterday, but can you tell me what was in the pockets?

If you can't hear it, is it still a sound?

Very high-pitched or very low-pitched sounds are hard or impossible for humans to detect, but they're still sounds. A young child's ears can detect frequencies of up to around 25,000Hz (Hertz, or cycles per second). This is the pitch made by bats hunting for insects to eat. As children get older their hearing becomes less sensitive – by the age of 13, most people can only hear sounds below 20,000Hz. The bats still fly overhead, but that 13-year-old might not be able to hear them. It doesn't mean they're not making a sound.

Adults who have abused their hearing by wearing headphones with the volume too high for too long, lose even more of the top frequencies. Some people can only hear sounds below 5,000Hz. Luckily, most of the sound energy in speech is in the range 300–3,000Hz, and so you can still communicate. Our ears are most sensitive to sounds around 3,000Hz which, incidentally, is the pitch of a crying baby. At the other end of the sound spectrum, very low-pitched sounds – below about 100Hz – feel more like a vibration than a note. If you walk past an electricity substation you will hear the low-pitched hum if you listen carefully, but you might feel it before you recognise it as a sound.

My grandad is a keen birdwatcher and I sometimes go out with him, but I can hear the birdsong much better than him. Why is this?

All humans, when first born, can hear sounds of about the same range of frequencies, but as you get older the ear gets stiffer and it cannot hear the higher sounds as well as it used to. Most birdsong is of high frequency and while your young ears are still flexible and sensitive, your grandad's are not. That's why older people will find it harder to hear birdsong. It also depends how loud the birdsong is. The loudness of a sound is measured in decibels (dB). A sound which is too quiet to hear has a loudness of 0dB. A sound ten times louder than this has an intensity of 10dB. A very loud sound, such a standing close to a jet plane taking off, can hurt. Generally sounds above 100dB are uncomfortable to the ear and at 130dB the sound will be painful. If you are chatting to friends the sound will be around 60dB.

Why are things harder to do when I'm tired?

It's due to changes in your muscles after long periods of activity. Your energy stores are reduced, and lactic acid builds up. As soon as you rest the balance is quickly restored, but that's just the physical side of feeling tired. Mental tiredness happens because the central nervous control is disturbed. Messages through your body travel slower, your thought and decision processes become clunky. That's why everything feels like really hard work.

Why do people get bags under their eyes when they're tired?

You get bags under your eyes when you're tired or ill. You can also get them if you have an allergy, or if you've been having a good weep at a soppy movie. Bags under the eyes are all to do with the movement of fluids in the body. We have some of the thinnest skin around our eyes, so any changes in the body fluid balance are going to show there first. It could be due to osmosis – the way fluids move through membranes which, in this case, are the cells in our body. Water in the body always travels from low-salt areas to high-salt areas, such as your eyes – tears are salty, aren't they? So perhaps that's what the body fluids are looking for, and why they hang around in bags under your eyes.

How is the information that reaches the eyes transmitted to the brain?

The photoreceptor cells are linked to a set of nerve cells in the retina, called bipolar cells. These link with a second type of nerve cell called ganglion cells. It is the nerve fibres of ganglion cells that take information from the eyes to the brain through the optic nerve.

Incidentally, we cannot see an object whose image falls on the retina at the point where the optic nerve leaves the eye. It contains no receptor cells, so any light striking this small area is not picked up. This is why we call it the 'blind spot'.

How does the brain turn those nerve signals into a picture?

The brain analyses all the bits of information it gets through the optic nerve. This process, called 'visual processing', is immensely complex, but it appears to be the occipital lobes at the back of the brain which deal with information from the eyes. Exactly how it works, though, remains one of the great mysteries of the brain.

Why do we have whites in our eyes?

If you compare us with other primates, such as apes and chimps, it's true that our eyes stand out much more, largely because of the white of the eye that surrounds the rest. In primates, the outer covering of eye, called the 'sclera', contains coloured pigments usually matching the colour of the rest of the eye, which makes them less obvious. In humans the sclera is white. We can only guess why this developed, but here's one theory – it helps us to determine more easily which way someone else is looking, and if they're looking at you or something else. It enables us to get a sense of whether other people are going to be helpful, or not. So perhaps we developed whites in our eyes as a form of social communication.

Is there such a thing as a bionic eye?

Yes there is, but for those born blind an artificial eye may not be all that useful, as their visual cortex – that part deep inside the brain which processes images – has not been trained to see.

For those who have lost their vision later on in life a bionic eye – which is an implant that replaces damaged retinal cells – may restore some of their sight. Retinal implants are constructed from twenty-five electrodes only 1/100th of a millimetre thick, and incorporate a miniature solar panel. When the panel absorbs light, tiny currents are generated in the implants which then stimulate the ganglion cells beneath, bypassing damaged retinal cells. So far the implants have worked in animals and in just one human volunteer. The patient was able to see a light shone in the eye, and could make out simple letters. If more electrodes are used, the picture might be even better, but there are many problems. They will need to make an implant that won't corrode in the salty solutions of the eye, and won't slice into the retina because the very thin implants are razor-sharp.

Why do we have ears, how do they work, and why have we got two of them?

We have ears to enable us to hear sounds – obvious, eh? But they have another important and less obvious job and that is to help us keep our balance. As far as hearing goes, the ear is a miniature receiver, amplifier and signal-processing system. It's divided into three parts: an outer ear, middle ear and inner ear, and is connected to the brain by the auditory nerve. Sound waves are collected by the pinna, which is the oval-shaped lump of skin on the side of your head, and channelled down into the ear canal. The air particles in the ear canal are made to vibrate and those particles at the end of the ear canal crash into the ear drum and make it vibrate as well. This vibrating flap of tissue is connected to three small bones in the middle ear called the hammer, anvil and stirrup, because that's what they look like. These bones act like small levers and couple the ear drum vibrations to the fluid-filled cochlea – this is where those vibrations are converted into signals for the brain to process.

For balance, there are three fluid-filled semicircular canals in the inner ear and they are set at right angles to each other. Inside the canals are sensory hairs, and these create signals that send impulses to the brain to stop you falling over.

What is taste?

We've got four basic taste sensations: sweet, salt, sour and bitter. To work out which is which you have receptor cells, located in 10,000 taste buds on the upper surface of your tongue, at the back of your throat, and a few in the roof of your mouth. Different bits of your mouth appear to react more strongly than others to particular taste sensations. The 'sweet' receptors are towards the tip of the tongue, which might be why we prefer to lick a lollipop. The bitter receptors are at the back of the tongue, and the sour down the sides.

But there might be more to taste than just sensations created on your tongue. Try this experiment. Get a friend and pinch their nostrils, then place a small slice of apple followed by a small piece of raw onion on the tip of their tongue. I bet they can't tell one from the other, and both will taste sweet. That's because smell and taste are closely linked. As much as 75 per cent of what we believe to be taste could actually be coming from smell. Have you noticed that if you have a cold and your nose is blocked, food tastes really dull? That's the reason.

An artificial nose, if such a thing could be invented, may have wide applications in medicine, and could be used to monitor changes in levels of environmental pollutants. More importantly, an artificial nose may well be capable of sniffing out how our own noses work.

Can we lose our sense of taste and smell?

Smell disorders are more common than taste disorders. Some people go to their doctor to say they've lost their sense of taste, but it can work the other way and it's possible for your sense of smell to go wrong and then you smell things (sometimes awful things) that aren't really there. Luckily, it's unusual to get both at the same time. Some people are born with poor senses of taste or smell, but most develop sense loss after an injury or illness.

Scientists have developed an easily administered 'scratch-and-sniff' test to evaluate the sense of smell. A person scratches pieces of paper treated to release different smells, sniffs them, and tries to identify each one from a list. In taste-testing, the patient responds to different chemical concentrations: this may involve a simple 'sip, spit, and rinse' test, or chemicals may be applied directly to specific areas of the tongue.

Why does my tooth tingle when I use a metal fork?

You've probably got a filling, and if you have, this is a well-known phenomenon and happens when a metallic object and a filling meet. If the object is made out of a different type of metal than the filling there will be something called 'galvanic action' between the two. This is an electrochemical reaction. If you bring two different metals together in an electrolyte, which in this case is the moisture in your mouth, electricity will flow between the two. Which way the current flows depends on the two metals and, if left alone, one metal will attack the other. So you get a very, very, tiny electric shock, which sets off the nerve endings in your teeth and that's what the tingle is.

There are several types of filling. The ones with metal in them might include mercury, silver, tin and copper and these are the strongest. On smaller or younger teeth fillings made of ceramic or powdered glass may be used. These, of course, won't give you that electrical tingle when your fork touches them.

Why does your mouth feel cold when you've just brushed your teeth?

You'll notice this more if you use toothpaste with mint or menthol in it. Chemicals in the mint stimulate neurones that register cold temperature, sending a message to your brain that something is cold. But the temperature of your mouth hasn't changed, the mint has simply confused the neurones, which have sent 'cold signals' to the brain. These nerves become sensitised so that if you have a drink shortly after brushing your teeth, these neurones will fire up again and send another cold signal to your brain, even if the water's not very cold at all.

What is instinct?

There are two sorts of behaviour – there's instinctive, or innate behaviour, and that is something we are born with, and then there's learned behaviour which develops as we grow up and comes from our experience of the world. A lot of behaviour appears without any previous experience. For example, the first time a wasp stuns a caterpillar, it uses precisely the right amount of poison injected into exactly the right spot. It's not learned how to do it, it just knows. This is instinct.

However, things are never as simple as they appear at first glance. Charles Darwin, the English naturalist who came up with the theory of natural selection, said that it applied as much to behaviour as it did to body parts. So, if a creature's genes do not allow it to behave in a way that will enable it to survive, it will not pass on those genes to the next generation.

But there are other ideas too. Some think that instinct is not 'driven from within' and rather it is feedback from the body that changes our behaviour. So, perhaps there is no such thing as instinct alone, and the way we behave relies on both inheritance and the effects of the world around us.

Why are bones hard?

All the soft and floppy tissues of the body are hung onto our bones, in the same way you hang clothes on a clothes hanger to make sure they stay in shape. Our bones have developed into the hard things they are so that they can support our soft tissues.

It is possible that at some time in our far distant past a few humans evolved with bones that were not hard, but try to imagine how you would manage if your bones were soft. Could you eat properly, or do your homework? Humans with soft bones simply are not as successful as hard-boned humans and so they wouldn't survive. Bones are a special type of tough connective tissue, and they are made so hard because there are large deposits of calcium and phosphorus compounds in them. This is why drinking lots of milk, which is full of calcium, is important if you want to grow up with healthy bones. But because we have been evolving for so long, our bones are much cleverer than you might think. If you looked very closely at a bone you would see it is full of spaces linked together in a certain way. Our bones are not just hard, they are also flexible and light. A piece of chalk and a bone are both made of calcium but would you want a skeleton made of chalk rather than of bones? Think how easily a stick of chalk snaps.

Why does blood turn a rust-like colour when it dries?

Blood contains small amounts of iron, and when exposed to the air it goes rusty. It's exactly the same reaction as when a screw goes rusty – iron meets oxygen in the air to produce brown iron oxide, which we call rust. But for the reaction to take place there has to be moisture as well and almost half of your blood consists of water.

Why do we poo every day?

Well, some people don't actually 'go' every day – anything from three times a day to once a week is considered normal. The reason we poo is to rid the body of undigested food. The actual process of releasing poo from the body is called egestion, or defecation.

Normally faeces (or poo) are composed of 75 per cent water and 25 per cent solids. Just less than a third of the solid matter is bacteria, another third is undigested food such as cellulose from plants, 10–20 per cent is cholesterol and other fats, 10–20 per cent is inorganic compounds such as calcium phosphate and iron phosphate and the rest (about 2 per cent) is protein. The protein comes mainly from cells on the inside of the intestine which are shed and picked up by the faecal mass as it travels towards the anus, but also from bile pigments and from dead white blood cells.

The brown colour of faeces is due to the breakdown products of bile pigments, one of which comes from the breakdown of red blood cells. Faeces smell because bacteria living in the waste break it down using many anaerobic chemical reactions. These produce compounds, such as indoles, hydrogen sulphide and mercaptans, which have strong and unpleasant odours.

How many cells are in the human body?

The best estimate is actually around 50 million million. However, that is an estimate. The number doesn't remain the same. Blood cells can divide in the body in response to different challenges, and therefore there is not a static cell count within any one person.

Why do wisdom teeth take so long to appear?

Teeth arrive in stages but always in the same order. Milk teeth arrive first, then incisors and canines as the milk teeth fall out, then first molars, then second molars, and finally wisdom teeth appear usually between the ages of 17 and 20. While all these events are going on, the jaw is growing steadily. The simple answer is that if wisdom teeth were to arrive any earlier, there just wouldn't be any space for them. Some people don't have enough room for them even then, and the new wisdom teeth are 'impacted', which means they clash with the previous molars and cannot emerge through the gum. That's when they have to be taken out. It is very rare for people to be born without wisdom teeth.

Wisdom teeth, these days, are thought of as 'vestigial' organs. That means they *were* an important part of our bodies as we evolved, but we haven't got much use for them now, and perhaps they will eventually disappear. Our early ancestors would feed on coarse, rough food, like roots and nuts, and would need strong teeth to break them down. We simply don't need that kind of chewing power any longer.

Why are there ridges on the roof of your mouth?

If your mouth were smooth then the food you were eating would slip around inside, and that would make it difficult to eat. If you look inside a shark's mouth you'll see that the ridges are much more pronounced, probably because the food it eats could still be alive and wriggling around a lot. The ridges help hold the food in place while the animal is biting and chewing.

Do you have muscles in your tongue?

Your tongue is just one big collection of muscles. There are three types of muscle in the body – skeletal muscles, involuntary muscles and cardiac muscles. Our tongue is a skeletal muscle, which gives us movement, and which we can control. This not only allows the tongue to move around when we are eating, but also secures it to the base of our mouth so there's no chance of us swallowing it. The tongue is also important in allowing us to form sounds, and therefore words. The tongue is a hard-working part of our bodies; it's part of talking, eating, tasting, and taking the temperature of food. All night it's pushing saliva down your throat so you don't wake up with a sodden pillow. Tongues deserve respect.

Why do your ears pop with changes in pressure?

When you go to a high altitude, or speed through a tunnel on a train, a change in air pressure takes place. This leads to a difference in pressure between the middle and the outside of the ear. This puts extra pressure on your ear drum, which could be damaging. To protect the ear drum, a mechanism has evolved to equalise the pressure. This involves a tube, called the Eustachian tube, which connects the middle ear to the back of your throat. The tube is opened by swallowing or yawning, which allows the pressure between the middle ear and the outside to become equal. The popping noise is caused by the pressure suddenly being released and the ear drum snapping back.

Why does your voice sound different when it is recorded?

We normally hear our own voices through the bones in our skull. But when you record your voice and then play it back, it sounds slightly different because you hear it through your ears. It can sound completely different. You may not even recognise yourself.

Does cutting hair makes it grow faster?

Cutting hair can't make any difference to it because hair is dead. Experiments have been conducted and it was found that hair didn't grow any faster no matter how often you shaved it off. Hair grows to a specific length and then it stops. That's why your eyebrows don't grow down over your eyelids. It's also why you might notice that a friend of yours has really long hair, but no matter how long you wait, yours won't grow any longer. The hair on your head is programmed to grow for a certain amount of time, then it stops, and stays there for a while before falling out. If you happen to cut it while it is in the growing phase it will keep growing, and that might make you think that by cutting it you were making it grow faster. But it would have kept growing at the same rate no matter what you did.

What are eyebrows for and why don't they grow longer?

Eyebrows are for protecting your eyes by deflecting water running down the forehead, and they're used in conveying facial expressions. They don't grow and grow because the hair follicles are genetically programmed to stop after about a centimetre of growth.

My brother has an eyelash which does not stop growing. How do some hairs know when to stop and others grow continuously?

As far as the long eyelash is concerned, the hair follicle or root itself is fine but the papilla, or growing hair, has got its instructions wrong. It's a glitch in your brother's genes, but it can be fixed. Hair goes through a cycle of growth and rest. The growth period lasts for 1,000 days and then stops. The hair follicle then rests. This is when your hair would normally fall out, and the resting period can last for 100 days. So, your brother's rogue eyelash should eventually fall out, and when regrowth starts the growing hair should have the correct instructions this time. With luck it will stop at the correct length.

Why does wee smell funny after eating asparagus?

This never used to be a problem until fertilisers started to be used in the late seventeenth century, when sulphur compounds began to be used to improve asparagus flavour. These sulphur compounds can also be found in vegetables such as cabbage, but the one in asparagus, known as 'asparagusic acid', doesn't break down when cooked in hot water. So your wee shouldn't smell after eating cabbage, but it will after eating asparagus. But these things are never quite as simple as they seem because some people will eat asparagus and not smell anything when they wee – that may be because they simply can't smell it, while others can.

How many muscles does it take to frown and smile?

It can take seventeen muscles to smile and forty-three to frown, although if you're mean you can just about smile using ten muscles; and six muscles will produce some kind of a frown. On average, they say frowning needs eleven and smiling needs twelve. Smiling uses less energy because we do more of it so the muscles are fitter. Interestingly, we are born with an ability to smile; it's not something we learn.

Why do your lips go dry?

The surface of our lips is different to the skin on the rest of our body. It mostly consists of a mucous membrane which has fewer and different glands than ordinary skin. Lips are also unlike other skin in that the outer layer is extremely thin, or completely absent in most people.

Lips also have almost no melanin, which is the natural pigment in skin that helps screen out the sun's harmful rays. As a result, moisture rapidly evaporates from the lips, causing them to dry out very easily. This dryness frequently results in chapping and cracking, and increases the risk of infection. This is made worse by the fact that they are very prominent and are generally unprotected by clothing and fully exposed to the elements. Exposure to sun, wind, cold and air-conditioned air can obviously speed the rate of moisture loss. This drying-out process can be made worse when you catch a cold or flu, or when you are suffering from hay fever, because you tend to breathe through your mouth when your nose is congested.

What's the speed of air through my nose when I sneeze?

A sneeze has more power in it than you might think. Believe it or not, the air through your nose when sneezing can reach over 100mph. Pain receptors in the cells which line your upper airways are triggered by dust or mucus, and these tell your brain to make you sneeze. The sneeze itself is just a very powerful out-breath. When the vocal chords close themselves, the pressure of air in the chest rises, and the air is then suddenly allowed to escape upwards towards the nose. If you think 100mph is a lot, did you know that when you cough the air can get up to 600mph?

What happens if you keep your eyes open when you sneeze?

It's physically impossible to keep your eyes open when you sneeze. This is a reflex action controlled by the autonomous nervous system, which is what controls your heart rate and breathing, and can't be consciously controlled. Your eyes will *always* shut when you sneeze. Don't try to fight it because you'll lose.

Why does a human drown while we have density slightly lower than water?

Drowning is a question of flooding the lungs, not necessarily sinking. For example, a baby can drown in a puddle of water a few centimetres deep, not because the baby doesn't float but because it has fallen face down in the water and it can't get up. Adults drown in the ocean because they swallow too much water, or exhaustion sets in and the person can no longer hold their head out of the water. Drowning isn't always to do with sinking.

Is it easier to float if you're fat?

The density of an average person is slightly less than the density of water so the average person just about floats. But no one is really average, so muscular people and skinny people with higher densities are poor floaters. Women typically contain more fat than men (15 per cent body fat compared to 10 per cent) and have lower densities, so are good floaters. The more fat you have, the less dense you are, and the more easily you will float.

Why do we sweat?

It's our way of controlling our body temperature. When the body is overheated, thermo-receptors in the skin send a signal to the temperature control region of your brain, which then sends signals to the sweat glands to produce sweat and transport it to the surface of the skin. Evaporation of the sweat from the skin cools it, and the body temperature drops. The sweat glands are deep in your skin and there might be as many as 2.5 million of them. The bit of the gland that makes the sweat is connected to a duct which runs up through the layers of skin to the surface, and these ducts are called the pores. Sweat doesn't smell when it's first released, but as soon as it reaches the surface of your skin it meets bacteria which start to grow, and that is what produces the odour.

Do we sweat underwater?

Yes! But obviously this sweating doesn't have the desired effect of cooling us down because the sweat doesn't evaporate; it just mixes with the bath water so you end up getting dehydrated and staying hot.

Why do some people hate hot weather and others think it is fine?

Because we all have different set temperatures. If, for example, my set temperature was 36°C I'd be more sensitive to higher temperatures than someone with a 38°C base. There is also a difference between men and women. Even though men and women do not have significantly different body temperatures, women tend to feel the cold more than men. Women generally have a slower metabolic rate (the rate at which they use energy) and so produce less heat. They also have less heat-generating muscle mass and so their shivering is less effective. Research has also shown that women cool down faster than men. Women also generally have a lower blood pressure than men, which means that there is less force driving the blood round the body. This means that women are often prone to cold hands and feet as there is not enough blood reaching the extremities.

How much heat is given out by the human body?

Curiously, men give out more heat than women. It's between 158 and 167 joules per square metre of skin in men, and 150–158 joules per square metre in women. Adult men have about two square metres of skin and so give out about 326 joules from their bodies each hour. If you're not certain how much a unit of energy (called a joule) is, at this power it would take 460 hours, or almost twenty days, to toast two pieces of bread.

Why do I always feel warm when my sister says she feels cool, even though we're in the same room?

Have you ever noticed that when you get hot your face goes red? Well, this is part of the body's way of cooling down – it lets blood flow into all the capillaries near the skin's surface so that you lose heat. This is called 'vasodilation'. Of course, the opposite happens if you are in a cold place. Then, in order to conserve heat, your body restricts the flow of blood to capillaries near the surface – this is called 'vasoconstriction'. It sounds as if your sister's body is simply not as efficient at this process as you are, so she has more trouble staying warm in cold weather.

Or there may be other reasons. Generally, a woman's thyroid gland works more slowly than a man's, so the body's rate of metabolism is lower. In other words, those processes of turning food into energy, and all the other chemical reactions that keep us alive, are happening more slowly and so not giving out as much heat. Women have less muscle mass too, which in turn reduces the body's energy production. Also women tend to have less body hair which makes them less insulated. So, there are good reasons why your sister may feel colder than you do.

Why do we use our elbows to test the temperature of babies' bath water?

Although there are more nerve endings in the hands and feet, the skin in these regions is usually quite thick and shields our skin temperature receptors from the heat we are trying to test. Also, our hands may have become conditioned to touching hot things. So, using a region of our body which has thinner skin is more effective. The elbow is probably used because it is easily dunked into the water.

What happens in our body when we fall down and hurt ourselves?

A whole army of chemicals swing into action to try and mend the damage and prevent further problems. If you are bleeding, chemicals regulating blood coagulation and inflammation will be released and there are dozens of these, including histamine which reduces blood pressure. This can lead to shock, which is a drastic reduction in the flow of blood round the body and can be life-threatening. Your adrenal gland will release stress hormones, and the chemical transmitters that signal pain will start to work. Also, psychological reactions to stress will come into play. In short, just about every physiological system in the body comes to life when it is under attack.

Why do you get a lump when you bump your head?

Our bodies have a way of trying to cope with disease or physical harm, and for this they use something called the immune system. If you fall and bump your head, some of the cells where you hit your head get damaged. So the immune system sends helper cells to take nourishment to that part of your head, and

at the same time carry away any waste from those cells. It is all these helper cells clustered around the bump that make it swell up. Don't worry if you get a lump like that, it's all part of the body trying to mend itself.

What is phantom pain?

Phantom pain happens when you feel the sensation of pain but the nerves aren't actually sending any pain signals to the brain. Pain nerves travel to the spinal cord where they make contact with spinal nerve fibres which send pain signals to the brain, but as the messages travel through the fibres they can be modified. Painkillers, for example, block the production of prostaglandins (a group of chemicals important in dealing with injury and illness) so that the pain signal cannot be triggered. In the spinal cord, the strength of the pain in the fibres can be reduced by endorphin-containing nerves – these are what are stimulated when you rub an injury to make it feel better. But if you were unlucky enough to have an accident and you lost, say, your leg, the endorphin-containing nerves would be lost too and so would their soothing effect. So you'd feel a pain in your leg even if your leg wasn't there and this is phantom pain.

Can hypnosis replace sleep?

No hypnosis cannot replace sleep. You cannot dream under hypnosis, and as dreaming is thought to be an important aspect of sleeping, hypnosis can never replace sleep. Hypnosis is not a form of sleep. What exactly it is, however, isn't known, although we understand that it is not a 'sleep-lie' trance as it is often described. It would be better to say it was a state of focused awareness and heightened suggestibility. Fifteen per cent of people are reckoned to be very responsive to hypnotism, and children tend to be very easily hypnotised. About 10 per cent of people will be impossible to hypnotise.

Why do people lie?

Tough one. It's probably part of our evolution and goes way back. Studies with chimps have shown that they are able to deceive each other, so perhaps it's been around a long time. Lying is a kind of self-preservation and protection, and you can even lie to yourself and make yourself believe things that are not true. We might lie about our exam results to gain more respect, which puts us in a stronger and therefore safer position – self-preservation again. We also kid ourselves that we'll never be found out, which is why lying can be dangerous too.

Children cannot lie when they are born, but as they learn language they learn about deception which will help them to survive in society. Lying becomes a very powerful tool, and the ability to lie with success (from your point of view) is reckoned to be one of our most advanced brain functions. It helps us succeed in love, war and business.

Interestingly, sufferers of autism cannot lie or understand deception.

Why do teenagers have spots on their faces?

Spots, or 'acne' to give them their proper name, are an inflammation of oily glands in the skin. These sebaceous glands produce a waxy substance called sebum which helps to waterproof the skin and keep it flexible. It's during puberty, or the teenage years, that these glands can go into overdrive and produce too much sebum, which blocks the pores and causes a build-up under the skin. This is what makes the dreaded spots. The sebaceous glands are controlled by the hormone testosterone which is released during puberty. In girls the testosterone comes mostly from the adrenal gland, whilst in boys it comes from the testes. Whilst acne will often clear itself as the amount of testosterone drops, about 5 per cent of people may need treatment from their doctors. The best advice for spots is 'don't touch 'em, don't squeeze 'em and don't pick 'em!'

Does nose-picking give you nose cancer?

Nose-picking is manually removing dried mucus coming down your nose. The mucus itself is useful because it is a way of getting rid of rubbish like bugs and dust and it is a natural process. But it can be a bit irritating when it dries and builds up, so it helps to clear it physically. Nose-picking is one way to do it. To do any damage to the inside of your nose, you would have to be a pretty committed picker over a number of years because the tissue inside the nose, the epithelium, is very rapidly renewed. As far as causing cancer goes, it's so improbable that picking your nose could cause it that you can, more or less, say it is impossible.

Does my brain work like a computer?

Most certainly not, and biologists and psychologists can get annoyed when people assume that our brains work as if they were some kind of supercomputer. It is true that the brain consists of neurones but these are all connected in far more complex and subtle ways than the wiring in a microprocessor.

For a start, computers can only do one thing at a time while brains can do millions of things at once. In even the biggest computers, the wiring is still very simple compared to the connections within the brain. It might appear that the brain and the computer are trying to achieve the same result, but that doesn't make them the same kind of machine. To quote a well-known scientist, Steven Pinker, 'birds fly by the same physical laws that allow aeroplanes to fly, but that doesn't mean that birds and aeroplanes share a body plan'.

Which is faster – a human brain or a computer?

No existing computer can do all of the things carried out by the brain. The brain is hugely complex, with somewhere in the region of 50 billion neurones with a million billion synapses (or connections), and an overall firing rate of perhaps 10 million billion times per second. By comparison, a typical desktop computer is capable of the calculating power of a small snail, and the fastest supercomputer possesses the processing power of a mouse.

No computer can match the operation of the brain because no computer can rewrite its own program; all computer forms of 'thinking' are limited by the operating software. Only the human brain has the ability to step back, survey its own operation, and then decide what to do. This is possibly why human brains can be creative, whereas computers can't. Computers are very good, however, at doing simple, repetitive tasks. This is why they are better at doing calculations, especially involving large numbers. They can process information quickly, and without making mistakes – as long as they are programmed correctly!

Why do we get old?

A person starts to age a little from about 20, then more significantly from 40–50 onwards. Our body is continually

making new cells as older cells die, and when you are young, the number of new cells which are formed exceeds those that are dying. That's how we grow. But as we get older, the number of cells that die exceeds those which are being produced. The end result of all of this is that some of our organs start to function less well. Our muscles become weaker, our bones thinner, and mental function slows up. There's also the added problem that every time a cell is replaced and the DNA within the cell is copied, there's a chance that it can be damaged or mutated, in which case the new cell won't function properly.

Why can you knock somebody out if you punch them on the chin?

There are various weak points on the body which are more vulnerable than others. When these are hit, the effects will be more serious than if more well-protected areas are struck. The chin is one of these areas. Striking down upon the jaw will cause the jaw to break. Similarly, striking up on the end of the nose will break the nose. Other weak points on the head include the eyes, the bridge of the nose, the base of the skull, the throat and the carotid arteries (striking a carotid artery directly will cause a person to lose consciousness, because the blood supply to the brain is interrupted).

Weak points on the body include the kidneys, the solar plexus, the floating ribs, the knees, the groin, the wrist, the base of the spine, and the back of the ankle. What most of these weak points have in common is that they are either bones or joints that are vulnerable or could break easily, or areas where vulnerable organs are near to the surface of the body.

There are also pressure points, or nerve points on the body, where sensitive nerves are close to the surface. These sites are quite specific and often quite difficult to find, but there are examples in the elbow, behind the knee, along the collar bone, and behind the ears. I don't think that applying pressure to these sites would cause a person to become unconscious, but it is certainly very painful. Often followers of martial arts will learn about these vulnerable points of their bodies, so that they can learn how to defend them effectively.

Are Eskimos more hairy than other people?

You'd think so, wouldn't you, because it would help them to keep warm, but there's no evidence that they are. What they are very good at is insulating themselves with thick fur clothes. The secret of good insulation is to trap warm air next to the skin, and fur is very good at that. Inside, Eskimos are probably just as warm as someone living in the Mediterranean. The problem is their hands and feet, because even the thick mittens and boots that the

Eskimos wear are not enough to keep them warm. So, Eskimos do have better blood circulation in their hands and feet than other humans do. All the heat the blood brings to their fingertips has to come from somewhere, of course, and that makes the thick fur insulation even more important. Eskimos have a short, compact body shape with quite short arms and legs, and that also helps to minimise heat loss. People from hot countries, like Africa, tend to be much taller and thinner with longer arms and legs.

Why isn't there a cure for the common cold?

The common cold is caused by many different viruses, possibly as many as 200. At the moment we don't have any medicines to treat virus infections – actually, there are a few but they are far too strong to risk using them just to get rid of a cold. There is no vaccine for the common cold either – because so many different viruses cause it, it is impossible to zap them all. And anyway, a cold makes you feel a bit grotty for a few days and then you can fight it off without treatment, so a cure isn't really needed, although it would be quite nice sometimes.

Top tip – doctors now think the best way to avoid colds is by making sure you wash your hands regularly.

How does getting wet give you a cold?

The answer is it doesn't. Being wet and cold does not make you more susceptible to getting a cold. The common cold is a viral infection of the lining of the throat, sinuses and large airways. Many different viruses cause colds. Becoming chilled doesn't, by itself, cause colds or increase a person's susceptibility to infection by a respiratory virus. A person's general health or eating habits don't seem to make any difference either. Neither does having an abnormality of the nose or throat, such as enlarged adenoids or tonsils. However, people who are fatigued or emotionally distressed, and those who have allergies of the nose or throat, and women may be more likely to notice the symptoms of a cold.

So, why do there seem to be more colds around in cold weather? Possibly because in cold weather we tend to crowd together more, say in cafes or on buses. It might also be because cold, dry air makes it easier for the viruses to pass from one person to another, but that's only a theory.

Can you get a suntan if the Sun is shining through a window?

Ordinary window glass filters out most of the ultraviolet (UV) rays, and it's these which cause a suntan. Clothing has the same effect, which is why you cover up if the Sun is strong and you don't want to get burnt. The amount of UV that the glass filters out depends on the impurities in the glass. If there are iron impurities in the glass, then UV will get reflected rather than pass straight through the glass. Car windows in particular contain impurities to prevent the plastic inside cars from deteriorating. You can't get a suntan by sitting inside a car. Remember, glass only *reduces* the amount of UV coming through, it doesn't stop it completely. Don't think it's a substitute for sun-block.

Why does a small paper cut hurt so much?

This is a good example of why size *doesn't* matter and why a little cut can sometimes hurt more than a bigger one.

Our skin acts as the first line of defence to various pathogens determined to harm us. When this physical barrier is disturbed, the immune system kicks into action, bringing into play various chemicals, such as prostaglandins. These enlarge the blood vessels under the damaged skin and allow the skin to 'open up', helping white blood cells from the vessels to reach the wound. White blood cells attack and destroy any organisms trying to invade us.

Pain is a result of the stimulation of pain fibres. There are two kinds: A fibres and C fibres. A fibres are easily activated and are responsible for the sensation of touch; luckily for us these do not produce a high response. But when there is a cut, the major players are introduced – the C fibres. When they are 'turned on' (even if it is just a few of them in the case of a small cut like a paper cut), the impulses generated are significantly higher, so the pain feels stronger.

What percentage of an average fart is hydrogen sulphide?

Most of the air we swallow, especially the oxygen bit, is absorbed by the body before the gas gets into your guts, so by the time the air reaches the large intestine most of what is left is nitrogen. However, the bacteria in the gut also produce hydrogen and methane, and that's what makes up a fart. Farts vary depending on what you've eaten and how healthy your guts are, but on average a fart has 20–90 per cent nitrogen, 0–50 per cent hydrogen, 10–30 per cent carbon dioxide, 0–10 per cent oxygen, and 0–10 per cent methane. How long you hold in a fart makes a difference. The longer a fart is held in, the larger the proportion of odourless nitrogen it contains, and the smellier gases tend to be absorbed into the bloodstream through the walls of the intestine. A nervous person who swallows a lot of air and moves food through his digestive system rapidly may have a lot of oxygen in his farts because his body didn't have time to absorb the oxygen.

So, how much hydrogen sulphide there is in a fart will vary – but as we know, a little goes a long way!

How fast do your muscles grow?

The muscle grows in proportion with the rest of your body whilst you are growing up, but muscle also grows in mass and girth in response to exercise. The number of cells does not alter, but the size of these cells does. Within a few days of increasing muscle work, an increase in strength is noticed. This is due to the increase in neural drive; in other words you are learning to use the muscle. As the increased demands continue, protein synthesis is initiated, and additional proteins are incorporated into the existing muscle fibres, causing muscle growth. It can take as long as two months for the size of the muscle fibre to start growing. The exact speed at which the muscle grows is dependent on the individual and the amount and type of training undertaken.

How much skin do you shed in a day?

Humans are constantly shedding skin cells, and in one minute we shed 30,000–40,000 from our body. Each year this amounts to about 4kg of dead skin that gradually falls off as your skin rubs against materials next to it. The dead skin cells that fall off your body are normally the main constituent of dust in your home. Each day we shed approximately 11g of skin. This may sound a lot, but new cells are continually being formed to replace the ones that fall off.

The top layer of your skin, the part of it which you can see, is called the 'epidermis'. The epidermis is made up of four or five distinct layers of cells. The palms of your hands and the soles of your feet are normally exposed to greater friction than the rest of your body, so they have an extra epidermis cell layer. The epidermis on the palms of your hands and the soles of your feet is 1–2mm thick. The epidermis covering the rest of your body is made up of four layers of cells and is about 0.1mm thick. The dead skin cells fall off the top layer of your epidermis. The bottom layer of the epidermis contains cells which continually divide, producing new cells. These cells work their way up through all the layers of the epidermis a bit like people moving to the front of a queue. About two to four weeks after the cells have been formed they end up as dead cells and fall off.

What on Earth?

Spinning Earth
to floating clouds;
salty sea to breaking waves;
icebergs to nettle stings

How was the world created?

The entire solar system was formed from a massive ball of gas and dust. This dust slowly started to pull together under the effects of gravity, and the centre of the ball got hotter and hotter as dust bumped and stuck together. Eventually the central bit of this cloud got hot enough for the Sun to start burning. At this point the Sun 'switched on' like a fire suddenly igniting. This sudden switching-on blew a lot of dust and gas away from the Sun. So, in a sense you could say that the Sun did 'blow' the solar system into what it is today.

The whole thing also started spinning because of a law called the 'conservation of angular momentum'. This says that as something gets smaller, it spins faster and faster. So, as a spinning skater brings their arms into their body – and gets smaller – they speed up. Any slight rotation in the ball of dust and gas would have become bigger and bigger as it shrunk. As things spin, forces push the middle out and pull the top in. If you have a conker in the middle of a piece of string, hold each end and spin it round like a skipping rope, centrifugal forces will pull your hands in and push the conker out. The same happened with the ball of dust so that eventually it wasn't a ball any longer, but a disc surrounding the Sun. The planets then formed from this disc and so now all orbit in the same plane around the Sun.

Why is the Earth round?

All of the particles which make up celestial objects, such as our own Sun and Earth, are attracted to each other by the force of gravity and so they try to get as close to the common centre of gravity as possible. The object in which everything is as close to the centre as it can be, is a sphere. The Earth is not a perfect

sphere, though. Because of its rotation, it bulges at the equator by as much as 26 miles. So, rather than being a sphere, the earth is actually an oblate spheroid.

How much does the Earth weigh and how do we know this?

The Earth has a mass of 6×10^{24}kg. If you want to express it in tons it's about 6 with twenty-four zeros after it. We know this because of gravity.

Working out how much the earth weighs all goes back to the late eighteenth century, when Henry Cavendish first did an experiment to measure the force of gravity between two objects. Once you have that, and also the size of the earth (because for the purposes of the calculation you assume the mass of the earth to be located at its centre), you can do an experiment to measure the gravitational force that the earth exerts on, say, 1kg of material, and from this work out the mass of the earth.

Why don't we feel the Earth rotating?

We detect movement by observing our own position in relation to everything else, so if you are sitting in a car and driving along, you see the houses flash past – you know you are moving. But on the surface of the Earth, things which appear to stand still, like buildings and mountains, are really moving at the same speed as we are so we don't see any movement between us. But why don't we *feel* the movement – after all, the Earth is spinning at about 1,000mph at the equator?

It's because our bodies are very good at detecting changes in movement, but not movement itself. The body's internal way of telling it is moving has to do with the fluid in the semi-circular canals in our ears. This fluid moves around and helps us to balance. However, if we are moving at a steady velocity the liquid will remain in a steady position, just as it would if we were stationary. It is only when we decelerate or accelerate that the liquid moves relative to the ear and we sense that we are moving. In the case of the Earth, its speed of rotation is pretty constant so we ignore it. As an example, you can be quite happily reading a book on a plane that is flying fast and level, but as soon as it makes a turn you sense it.

What would happen to humans if the Earth stopped spinning?

One day the Earth *will* stop spinning, but it's a long way ahead, by which time human life will be long extinct and there'll be no one around to report on what happened. So let's imagine it.

For a start, if the Earth came to a sudden halt there would be a hell of a mess. Remember, the Earth is spinning at around 1,000mph at the equator and suddenly putting the brakes on at that speed would feel like a thousand times worse than running into a brick wall. Buildings would tumble, humans would be sent flying and not survive the impacts.

As far as the oceans are concerned, imagine you were towing a bath full of water at high speed down a road and suddenly came to a stop. The water, of course, would keep moving. If it were an entire sea that suddenly moved, imagine the results.

There would be no twenty-four-hour days because those are created by the spin of the Earth, and if the Earth stopped it would take a whole year for us to go round the Sun, while a day would be six months long, and so would the night. By daytime the temperatures would be baking hot, by night unbelievably cold. The seasons would disappear too. Add to that the loss of the ocean and atmospheric currents which are partly driven by the Earth's rotation, and you find that all our weather and season patterns have gone as well. So keep on spinning, please, Earth.

If the centre of the Earth is so hot, why isn't the ocean warmer?

You're right to say that the centre of the Earth is extremely hot – about 4,300°C – and that is largely due to radioactive activity in the Earth's core. But the amount of energy that travels from there to the Earth's crust is very small in relation to the huge amount of water that has to be warmed up. In fact the crust of the Earth – the bit round the outside on which we live – can be quite cool if it isn't near any volcanic areas, and the deepest waters, which are in direct contact with the crust, are even colder – deep sea temperatures can be as low as 2°C.

Is the weight of the world increasing or decreasing?

The Earth catches around 500 tons of dust and stones from space every day, so in its 4-billion-year history it has put on about 16 million, million, million tons in weight. This only actually accounts for less than 1 per cent of the Earth's total mass so, although it sounds a lot, it's not much really. But it's true that the Earth has gained weight over the years.

Why don't buildings fall over?

The stability of any structure depends on three things: its weight, its height, and the size of its base. A tall, thin structure with a small base is less stable than a short structure with a large base. That's why a pencil balanced on its end is easier to knock over than a cup. But the weight distribution makes a difference too, so if most of the weight of a tall structure is close to the ground and within the base, then it will be more stable than a tall structure which has its weight evenly spread.

Buildings fall down when something called 'structural failure' occurs. This is what can happen to bridges over wide rivers in very high winds. The strong gusts of wind apply loads to the bridge which cause parts of it to break and the whole structure collapses. When we build structures, we usually need to make sure that they will not fail and fall down and to ensure this we build them strong and stiff. A strong structure can withstand the intended load without breaking, and a stiff structure will not change shape when its load is put on. If it doesn't break and it doesn't change shape, it will remain standing. Even so, we still have to build it in such a way that it can cope with the unexpected. If we designed a bridge just able to cope with the weight of ordinary cars and lorries, we would be in trouble if there was a very high wind, or a very large snowfall. So we build them stronger than you might expect. Engineers call this the 'factor of safety'.

So what exactly is a stable structure?

The weight of any building is due to the force of gravity pulling down vertically on the mass of it. There's an imaginary place within each structure through which we imagine the force of gravity to act, and that's called the centre of gravity. If the position of the centre of gravity is low and is well inside a large base area, then the object is said to be very stable. If the centre of gravity lies to one side of the base area, the object is much less stable. If the centre of gravity is outside the base area, the object is very unstable and may require further support. A tall object tends to be unstable because its centre of gravity is in a very high position, which means that the object doesn't have to move very far from the vertical before the centre of gravity falls outside its base area, and over it goes.

Which metal is the strongest in the world?

The strength of a metal depends on the grain size of the metal. The smaller the grain size, the stronger the material is. For physical strength, steel is recognised as one of the strongest and most important materials that we use. It is composed of iron, with a small percentage of carbon. The carbon atoms position themselves between the layers of iron atoms and this gives added strength because it is not so easy for the iron atoms to 'slide' over one another. The percentage of carbon in the steel can be altered during the making of it, and it is this which has an important effect on the grain structure and hence the strength of the steel. Although it makes the steel stronger, it does make it more brittle, which means it can snap or crack more easily.

Metals such as titanium and aluminium have extremely high strength-to-weight ratios, meaning they are very strong but still very light compared to steel, and are used in space and in aircraft for this special property.

How hot is oil when it comes out of the ground?

It varies a lot. For example, oil from the Oola field in the Norwegian North Sea is about 160°C when it comes up from 3.6km down. Oil from the Forties field in the British North Sea comes from only 2.6km deep and is at about 96°C. So, it all depends on the depth the oil comes from – the deeper, the hotter.

When an animal or plant grows, is more matter coming into the universe?

No, it's all recycled. It may take an incredibly long time but it's all going round in one big circle. For example, when something dies, then fungi or bacteria will cause it to decompose and that will release the matter to be used again. It may become trapped in the Earth's crust, as dead trees do, and over thousands of years turn into coal. When the coal is burnt it will release carbon dioxide into the air, making it available for growing plants to use. And so it goes on, round and round.

Why are some clouds flat on top?

The atmosphere can have several layers in it. These can be at different temperatures and where winds travel at different speeds. If the tops of large cumulus clouds reach a layer where the wind is travelling faster than in the layer below, the tops of the clouds will be sheared off. The most common type of cloud in which this happens is the flat-topped cumulonimbus, which often brings lightning and heavy rain.

Why do some clouds produce rain and not others?

Clouds are made of tiny water droplets. Once the number of droplets in the cloud becomes high, larger water droplets form. Eventually, these droplets become large enough that the force of gravity acting on them overcomes the forces which keep them in the sky (these forces arise from the upward movement of air molecules) and they fall as rain. But if the droplets don't reach the right size, they'll stay up there and not fall as rain.

Why does it snow?

In cooler areas of the world, away from the equator, clouds can stretch up into air which is below freezing. Clouds are a mixture of water droplets, ice crystals and special supercooled water droplets, which are droplets of water that are still liquid even though they are below freezing. The coldest part of a cloud is nearest the top. At the bottom, a process called 'coalescence' is going on – this is when millions of tiny water droplets collide to form bigger droplets, which in turn collide, forming bigger ones and so on. Higher up, a process called 'accretion' is going on.

The ice crystals attract the supercooled droplets, which freeze onto them. As the crystals grow and stick to others, snowflakes form. When they become heavy enough, they start to fall as snow. Of course, snow will only make it to the ground if the temperature is below freezing all the way from the cloud to the ground, otherwise all you get is rain.

What causes wind?

The sun heats the air in some regions more than in others. This causes it to expand and become less dense. Less dense air is 'lighter' and rises, creating low pressure in the area below because of a reduced weight of air pushing down. More air rushes in from the nearest high pressure area to fill the gap and it is this movement of air that you feel as wind.

Why do you sometimes get a mist rising off the ground after it has rained?

For a start, the surface onto which the rain has fallen has to be warm enough to cause some of the rain to evaporate, or turn into water vapour. Air can only hold so much water vapour, and how much depends on things like temperature, humidity and air pressure. If the evaporating rain 'fills up' the layer of air above it, some of that water vapour will condense out and appear as mist.

Why do clouds float?

Clouds are made up of tiny water droplets and these droplets fall to earth with different speeds depending on how big they are. But these droplets are so small that turbulence in the air, which occurs in clouds, holds them up. This is why clouds float. When water droplets in the clouds get too big to be held up by the wind turbulence they fall to the ground. That's when you get rain.

Why are clouds different shapes?

As moist air rises, it expands and cools. Cooler air can hold less moisture and eventually the air reaches a point where the moisture condenses out and clouds form. The shape of a cloud depends on how the air was lifted, how quickly, and what its temperature was. Air rising over a city will often form cumulus clouds, while stratus clouds are formed by hot air rising over cold air.

Why don't clouds blow away in the wind?

The wind does, of course, blow clouds along. You can see them skidding across the sky, and the wind is very important in determining the shape of clouds. With thunderstorms, for example, you get winds that blow upwards inside the clouds, making them all puffy and tall.

Clouds are formed from drops of water that have condensed around 'seeds'. These are minute bits of dust and dirt in the atmosphere. Water doesn't just make drops on its own; it has to have these seeds to start things off. You also have to have exactly the right temperatures and pressure. So clouds will only form where all of these conditions are dead right, and it doesn't matter how windy it gets, the cloud won't go outside of the boundary where these conditions occur.

If clouds are made of air and water, why can you see them?

If you look at the water coming from a kettle when it boils, or your breath on a cold day, you can see the water vapour. The water present in a cloud is water vapour. What happens is the water evaporates (turns from liquid to gas) and rises in the cloud until it meets the cold air higher up. This makes it condense and gives it the same white appearance as steam from a kettle, but this time we call it clouds.

Why do storm clouds look darker than normal clouds?

Something appears white if it reflects all the wavelengths of light in the visible spectrum. That's what is happening in a white cloud – the water droplets in it are reflecting all the Sun's rays. But storm clouds have more water vapour in them, and the droplets are larger and packed more closely together. So, instead of being easily reflected, the light scatters and less of it gets through. This makes the cloud look darker. As the droplets get larger, as in a growing storm cloud, so the cloud gets blacker. That's why dark clouds overhead are a sign of rain – it's because the water droplets are getting bigger, shutting out more light, and sooner or later they're going to have to fall.

Why do clouds form in some parts of the sky and not others?

It's because the atmosphere is not a uniform place. If a particular piece of air has the required amount of water vapour in it, a raindrop will form (usually). But even just a few centimetres away, the amount of water vapour can be completely different and not enough to produce a raindrop. On top of that, you need something for the raindrop to form around, such as a piece of dust, a bit of pollution, a spot of volcanic ash, or whatever. The condition of the atmosphere can be completely different from metre to metre. There might be slightly different wind conditions, or pressure. No two areas of air are the same. Clouds will only form where the conditions are just right for the water vapour in the air to condense out, and conditions might be perfect in one place, and no good just a few metres away.

How do we know snow crystals are unique?

Although it's often said, you can't prove that all snow crystals are unique because we can't examine every individual one. However, we can say that there are many millions of different shapes that snow crystals can form, so it's unlikely that you'll find two that are identical. The size and shape of each snow crystal depends on the temperature and amount of water in the air around them. This is constantly changing as they form, so their shape is very complex and changes even as it's forming. And because it's the air very close to the snow crystal that matters, even two snowflakes forming right next to each other will be different. It's been estimated that a trillion, trillion snowflakes fall from the sky every year, and nobody has found two identical ones yet.

Why does the temperature suddenly drop before dawn?

This might be more noticeable after a still, clear night when the weather isn't changing very much. The air temperature gradually drops as night falls and the ground loses heat that cannot be replaced by the Sun's rays, as it is during the day. This temperature falls throughout the night and can continue to fall even though the Sun has risen in the morning. At that point, the amount of incoming radiation is still less than the outgoing radiation, so the coolest part of the day is often around dawn.

Why is the sea salty?

When the Earth was young and the land and seas had just formed, the water in the seas was not salty, but then it rained on the rocks, which dissolved the minerals that made up the rocks. The rain, now with the dissolved minerals in it, made streams and the streams made rivers and headed for the sea. Eventually the rivers reached the sea, and there the water, and the minerals, stayed until the heat from the Sun evaporated the water. The minerals got left behind, while the water went back to being clouds and rain. Then the rain fell once more onto the rocks and washed more and more minerals into the sea. More evaporation took place, which meant more rain, which meant more minerals running into the sea, and the sea got saltier and saltier as you find it today.

Salt can get into the sea in other ways too. In many parts of the ocean, underwater volcanoes are constantly erupting, bringing salts with them. Also, hydrothermal vents can be found in parts of the ocean floor. This is where heated seawater emerges after travelling through gaps in the Earth's crust. These hot waters carry a lot of salt. If they emerge through rocks at surface level, we call them hot springs.

Why does the ocean appear to look blue?

Is it really blue? Not always. In Britain it's usually grey or green. The sea reflects the colour of the sky, so the sea is only blue when the sky is.

But there are other things that affect the colour of the ocean. Sometimes the minerals in the sea can affect the colour, but only locally. Certain seaweeds or algae in the water can even make the water look red. The colour of the sea floor has some effect too: marl is a light-coloured mineral that reflects the light off the sea floor so that it appears much bluer than normal. This is because seawater is naturally a very pale blue colour. When light passes through it and is reflected back, a lot of red and green light is absorbed and only the blue light is transmitted. Places like these are quite rare, and so the main reason the sea is blue is because it reflects the colour of the sky, and the sea looks bluest when there is a clear blue sky.

Why are the ripples in the sand always on the bit of the beach nearest the water?

Ripples on a beach are caused by the waves in the water when the tide comes in, and so they'll only be found on sand that was covered in water earlier in the day. Sand also dries out quite quickly once it is exposed, and any ripples that might have been preserved are soon lost. If you've ever tried making a sand castle with dry sand you'll know how difficult it is to get the sand to maintain any shape you give it, but add some water and the castle-building is much improved. Nearer the low water mark, further down the beach, the sand is still wet and holds its form longer. So the recent ripples are usually only seen in wet sand or in sand that is at least still damp enough to hold its shape. That's always the sand nearest to the sea.

Why does a sea wave break?

It trips over its own feet. As a wave approaches the shore, it moves slowly into shallower water. Eventually, it starts to feel some friction between the moving water and the seabed beneath it. This causes the lower layers of water to slow down. But the upper lays are not slowed to the same degree, so the top of the wave keeps on moving while the lower part drags its feet. Eventually, the top has to collapse and fall over itself, and that's when you get a breaking wave.

What are icebergs made of?

Although you find icebergs floating in the sea, in fact they are mostly made of fresh water. This is because icebergs are not frozen seawater but lumps of ice which have broken off glaciers which had slid into the sea. Glaciers are made of compacted snow, which comes from fresh water. Icebergs can be many hundreds of miles long. An average iceberg will survive for three or four years before it drifts into warmer water and melts.

Why do you hear a noise when you hold a seashell to your ear?

If you are near the sea, the noise you hear is the noise of the sea which your ear is picking up, not only from the inside of the shell but all around you. But suppose you're miles from the sea, where does the rushing sound come from then? When sound hits a hard surface, the angle it bounces off at is the same as the angle it hits at. That means that any sound that enters a cavity, such as a shell, gets trapped and rebounds several times, which acts to amplify the sound. What you are hearing then is

the sound all around you that creeps into the shell and bounces around. The size of the shell determines which frequencies are amplified more than others – you'll hear a higher-pitched hiss with a small shell than with a larger one.

Why does wind blow in gusts?

Wind is caused by air moving from an area of high pressure to an area of low pressure. The surface of the Earth is not the same all over – it has hills, valleys, mountains and oceans. Some of these surfaces produce more friction than others. So wind does not flow smoothly from place to place. In cities and towns, which are some of the roughest areas as far as friction is concerned, winds gust the most. Higher in the atmosphere, the effects of the Earth's surface are minimal and the wind speed is more constant. Gusts of wind are like waves – they don't travel continuously through the air and might be blowing one minute and disappear the next.

How does a nettle sting you?

The underside of a nettle leaf carries a collection of hairs which are, in fact, hollow tubes made out of silica – not unlike glass tubes. When you brush against a stinging nettle, the tiny hairs on the surface of the leaf are broken, leaving a sharp end, a bit like a hypodermic needle, and this introduces a chemical called acetylcholine into the surface of the skin. It also introduces some histamine which causes the itching. The acetylcholine will be absorbed directly into a nociceptor, which is nerve cell in the skin that sends messages to the brain. The result is the painful stinging sensation.

Not all nettles sting. There is one variety, *Urtica dioica*, which produces no acetylcholine. The sting can also vary from season to season. The sting is usually strongest in the spring because that's when you find most young nettles, which produce more of the irritating chemicals.

Nettles have many uses; the young leaves and shoots are rich in vitamins and minerals and are cooked as greens, and brewed for beer or an iron-rich tonic tea for anaemia. The leaves are a valuable fertiliser, while the plant is a diuretic, digestive, astringent, stimulates circulation and clears uric acid, relieving arthritis, gout and eczema. A nettle poultice treats eczema, burns, cuts and haemorrhoids, and the seeds were given for tuberculosis and to treat the lungs after bronchitis. So, stinging nettles do have their uses apart from stinging you. Incidentally, heating or drying the leaves removes the sting.

Why don't Christmas trees lose their leaves in the winter?

A tree uses its leaves not only for collecting light but also to exchange gases such as CO_2 (carbon dioxide) and water vapour. Deciduous trees shed their leaves in winter to slow down their water loss. Conifers – and Christmas trees are conifers – can keep their leaves because the leaves are designed to retain water. They have a much smaller surface area and are coated in a thick, waxy skin which stops water from evaporating. Because of that, they can keep their leaves all year round.

Why do leaves change colour?

Leaves are clever things. It's where trees get all their food from. First of all they take water from the ground and carbon dioxide from the air. They then use sunlight falling on the leaves to turn those two into oxygen and glucose, which is what the trees live on. That's called 'photosynthesis' and part of the process uses a chemical called chlorophyll, which is green. This is what makes the leaves green. Trees, somehow, know when winter is coming – probably due to the shorter daylight hours – and start to shut down. The photosynthesis comes to a halt and with it the need for chlorophyll. Then the greenness disappears, and we are left with red and brown leaves. In fact, the red and brown was there all the time, it's just that in the summer there's so much chlorophyll that you can't see it.

If it's 12 noon here, what time is it at the South Pole?

International time zones run along the lines of longitude which meet at the North and South poles, so it would seem that at the poles all time zones would meet. In a way, they do, but the poles don't fall into any time zone. Imagine that you are standing at one of the poles where all those time zones meet, and imagine all the lines spreading out from under your feet. You could argue that the time would change depending on which direction you looked. Of course, that would make life impossible, so it's agreed that the time is the same as GMT. So if it is 12 noon GMT in Britain, it is also 12 noon GMT at the South Pole

Why and how do petals open?

Plants can't move around much, so they have to rely on other methods to reproduce and create new plants – it's called pollination. Pollen is basically the male sex cells of the plant and consists of tiny grains formed by the stamens of a flower. These can be carried in the wind, or by insects, to the ovaries of another flower, which is the female part of the flower. When this happens, the plant is fertilised. Petals open only when a flower is ready to be pollinated, and the petals are there to attract suitable pollinators. That's why plants have brightly coloured petals. Yellow is very attractive to insects, especially bumble bees. However, it costs the plant a lot of energy to make these petals and so they will only open for a short time. There are certain triggers, such as temperature, which the plant will recognise as being the right time to attract insects, and so the petals will open. No one's really sure quite how this happens, but it seems that physiological changes in the water pressure in the plant are involved in the opening process.

Does talking to plants help them grow better?

Many people think so, but others think they are a bit mad. In fact, it's just possible there may be some truth in it. Plants grow better when they have more carbon dioxide. The level of carbon dioxide in ordinary air is quite low, but the air we breathe out has a lot more. If you talk to a plant, you breathe on it, giving it extra carbon dioxide. However, to have any real effect, you would probably have to talk to the plant for several hours each day, and that *would* be a bit mad.

What is the difference between sand and quicksand?

Quicksand is made of normal sand, but it is loosely packed and it is mixed with such a high proportion of water that it is very runny. The reason you sink into quicksand is because it is not strong enough to bear your weight. The problem with quicksand is that you can't get out of it very easily because there is nothing for you to put pressure onto in order to push yourself out. Imagine trying to get out of a patch of quicksand; you would try and push down with your feet or hands, but every time you push downwards you end up sinking further as the quicksand is too runny to be able to put up any resistance to your pushing. Down and down you go.

Why don't fish get electrocuted by lightning?

Lightning is very high in voltage but low in current. The ocean is such a large volume of water compared to the current that the electrical discharge is way too small to electrocute anything. In other words, when lightning hits water it dissipates in every direction at a time so the actual charge per unit of water is quite low. Mind you, if you had big fish in a really small pond and lightning struck, you probably would end up with cooked fish!

Science in my Life

Batteries to bar codes;
toothpaste to Post-It notes;
bursting bubbles
to burning candles;
swallowing spiders
to keeping warm

Why can you only fold a piece of paper seven times?

It is often said that if you take a piece of paper and start to fold it, then you can never get further than seven folds. Well, it's sort of true. The problem is the strength of paper. A large sheet of paper cannot be made thin enough to be folded more than seven times without being so thin it falls apart. Thick paper, by the way, won't even fold seven times. If you take something stiff, like card, you can only fold it two or three times.

The other problem is that the number of layers doubles with each fold, so after six folds you have sixty-four layers. That means that if you want to try for seven folds you are going to have to create 128 layers, which requires a lot of strength, and probably distorts the paper. However, if you started with a huge sheet of paper, the proportion of fold to paper is much smaller and you may be able to get as far as eleven folds before it becomes impossible. Students in the USA claim to have got as far as thirteen folds. A stronger, more flexible material can be folded more than seven times. For example, if you took a large sheet of fine silk you could easily fold it seven times and more.

Why is a paper napkin easier to tear when it's wet?

If you tear a paper napkin in half and look very closely at one of the torn edges you'll see that there are lots of fibres sticking out from it. These are wood fibres, which is what is used to make paper. In a wet napkin, the water gets in between the fibres and makes them slippery, and when you tear it, rather than break they slip over each other. In a dry napkin this doesn't happen and so you must actually break the fibres to tear the napkin, which takes more effort. There is an experiment you can do to show how these slippery fibres change the way paper behaves when wet. Compare the number of times you can fold a sheet of dry paper, with the number of times you can fold a wet sheet. The difference is to do with the slippery fibres.

What's the difference between digital telephones and an old-fashioned one?

When you speak into an older telephone, a small microphone turns your voice into an electrical signal which matches your voice – an analogue signal – which then travels along the wires connecting you to the person you are calling. At the other end, an earpiece turns those signals back into sound. That's how 'old-fashioned' phones work.

With a digital phone, a processor takes those same electrical signals from the microphone but converts them into a binary signal which consists of zeros and ones – nothing else. At the receiving end, a processor takes this stream of zeros and ones and turns them back into sound. There's an advantage with this. The processor at the receiving end can look at the information it is receiving and, by comparing it with its own programs, can decide if any of the information it contains is missing. If so, it can replace it. This gives a clearer signal.

What colour is the light in a fibre optic cable?

Near infrared light is used in fibre optic cables, which is just beyond the visible spectrum, so you wouldn't be able to see it. The light in a fibre optic cable travels along the fibre by being reflected off the inside surface of the fibre itself, as if it were travelling down a tube which had a mirrored inside surface. This is how it can travel round bends and achieve long distances –

up to 60 miles. The light uses a very important effect which is called 'total internal reflection'. This happens when a beam of light meets a boundary at such an angle that the light is reflected rather than passing through. You can see this effect if you try swimming under water. If you look up, the surface of the pool will appear to be a mirror.

Optic fibres can carry huge amounts of information – as much as 3 million phone calls or 90,000 television channels at the same time. You couldn't do that with copper wires.

Where does electricity come from?

Electricity is energy, and energy is what makes things move or change. So when we switch on a light, we are changing electrical energy into light and some heat. But if we go way back in the chain, all the way to the power station, what we find there is another form of energy transfer.

Coal is made up of plants that lived millions of years ago. When they died they were gradually buried under tons of rock and the huge pressures changed them into coal, and they became a form of compressed energy. We release that energy by burning it. This gives us heat, another form of energy, which we use to boil water to make steam, which drives a turbine that makes it into mechanical energy. This mechanical energy in turn drives a generator which produces electricity, another form of energy.

What is the speed of electrons down a copper wire?

The energy carried by electrons down a piece of copper wire is called 'electricity'. So, how fast do those electrons have to move to get from the power station to your house? Not as fast as you may think. Electrons actually move quite slowly along power cables. They drift rather than race along. How they get the energy from the power station to your homes is by transferring it from one electron to another, a bit like a relay race. And this can happen very quickly. Electrons randomly move around in metal wires anyway, without actually going anywhere – rather like running on the spot. When put in an electric circuit, these electrons then start to drift along, but at the sedate speed of about 3m per second, although the electrons themselves will be buzzing around wildly.

Why do electricity pylons buzz?

The buzz happens because of the kind of electrical current pylons carry, which is AC – alternating current. This means the electricity is reversing its direction of flow quite rapidly when the current is pushed down the wire, then pulled back, then pushed down again, and so on. With mains electricity, the full cycle of push–pull and back to push again happens fifty times each second, and that's called a frequency of 50 Hertz (Hz).

When an electric current flows through a wire it creates some magnetism, and things around the wire including the wire itself are affected by the magnetic field. With AC that magnetism is changing all the time, so things are pushed one way then the other fifty times a second, in rhythm with the changes in the current. This sets up a vibration if the object that is being affected is of the right shape and size – usually big and heavy, like a transformer or a pylon. That vibration in turn produces sound. The sound they make is at the same frequency as the current, 50Hz. It's a rather low note and it's the constant buzz you hear.

Why do batteries that are running down, recover slightly if you don't use them?

In a simple copper–zinc battery, a copper plate and a zinc plate sit in a dilute sulphuric acid solution. When the battery is working, small bubbles of hydrogen gradually form around the copper plate and prevent the flow of charge. When the battery is disconnected, some of the hydrogen disperses slightly. When you use the battery again, there is less hydrogen to block the flow of electrons for a short while and the battery will work again. But soon the hydrogen builds up and again the battery doesn't work. That's when you have to buy another.

What's the click when an electric kettle switches off?

You are hearing the sound of a bimetallic switch which has reached a certain temperature. It means the kettle has boiled, and so has disconnected the power from the kettle. The switch is made from three pieces of metal brought together like a sandwich, and they expand at different rates when heated up. They are often copper (or brass) and steel. Each has a different so-called 'coefficient of expansion'. As the kettle comes to the boil and the strip warms, one of the metals expands more than its neighbour and this causes the whole strip to bend. As it bends, it breaks the electrical circuit and switches the kettle off.

Bimetallic strips have other uses. They can be used in mechanical clocks to ensure that they keep precise time when room temperatures are changing.

When an electric bell rings, electrical energy is converted into sound energy. But if the bell is placed in a vacuum, no sound is heard. What happens to the energy?

The energy from the power source is first converted into kinetic energy, which drives the hammer that hits the bell. The bell then vibrates, which causes the air molecules next to it to vibrate, and so a transfer of energy takes place. In air, the transfer of energy to the air molecules means the bell eventually stops vibrating – it runs out of energy. But in a vacuum this means of losing energy is not there. However, there are other ways the bell can lose energy. Some of it is converted into heat. This also happens when the bell rings in the open air, but in a vacuum more energy is lost this way as there is no air to provide damping.

What are LEDs?

Light emitting diodes (LEDs) are solid state semiconductor devices, like transistors. Unlike an ordinary light bulb, they don't have a filament that will 'burn out' and so they have a huge life, consume very little power, and produce far less heat. You see them everywhere: on digital clocks, television screens, anywhere you need a small and reliable indicator bulb. They work because of the movement of electrons between different energy levels in atoms. If an electron falls to a lower energy level, then to conserve energy, light in the form of a photon is emitted. The colour of the light depends on the difference between the two levels of energy. For an LED to appear red requires the photon of light to have the wavelength we recognise as red. The semiconductors used to make an LED are chosen to ensure the light emitted is the colour that is required. In theory, any colour of LED is possible as long as you can find a material that has a suitable energy gap to produce a photon of the right wavelength.

How do LCDs work?

LCD stands for 'liquid crystal display'. Liquid crystals were discovered more than 100 years ago by two scientists, Friedrich Reinitzer and Otto Lehmann, who saw that certain pure compounds went a strange, cloudy colour when they melted. They said that this was a fourth 'state of matter'. Usually there are three states of matter – solid, liquid and gas. Water can change from being one or the other by being heated or cooled. But this cloudy behaviour, they thought, was different, so they said it was a new state of matter called the 'liquid-crystalline' state of matter. Certain materials turn into this state at precise temperatures, and can flow like a liquid but still keep an ordered structure, which is what crystals usually have.

Crystals are usually made so that their atoms and molecules line up. In a liquid, this structure is usually lost, but not in these strange materials which behave like both a liquid and a crystal at the same time. The materials used in LCDs have molecules that are all lined up in one direction but this direction can be changed by an electric or magnetic field. It does not require a huge amount of power to do this, which is one reason why LCDs have become used in computer and television screens. By changing the direction the molecules point in, you can either let polarised light through, or not. If not enough light gets through, this produces black, or varying shades of grey depending on how much light is allowed to pass.

Why do people in my photos always have red eyes?

You only get red-eye photos if you're using a flash. The reason you are using the flash in the first place, of course, is because you are trying to take a picture where the light levels are low. This means that the pupils in your subject's eyes will be wide open – the pupil is what controls the amount of light going into our eyes. When the flash fires, the burst of light enters the eye through the wide-open pupil and falls on the retina at the back of your eye. This is the light-sensitive part of the eye and it is well supplied with blood vessels, so it appears red. Some of this light burst is absorbed by the retina, but not all of it. The 'red-eye' effect you see is the surplus light being reflected back to your camera through the wide-open pupil which has not yet reacted to the bright flash of light.

Some cameras claim to be 'anti red-eye'. These work by shining a light on your eyes just before the picture is taken. This makes the pupils contract so less light falls on the retina and so less red light is reflected back. If you were indoors, you could try to switch on as many room lights as possible in order to produce the same effect.

Why don't I fall out of a loop-the-loop fairground ride?

Imagine a ball on a piece of string. Hold the string in one hand and swing the ball around. There is a force acting along the string towards your hand which stops the ball flying off, and this is called the centripetal force. Newton's third law of motion says that for every action there is an equal and opposite reaction, and this is called the centrifugal force. When you're doing a loop-the-loop, the centrifugal force acts outwards, 'pushing' you into your seat so that you don't fall down. If you were to stop moving at the top of the loop, however, the centrifugal force would cease to exist and you would fall as a result of gravity unless you were strapped in very well.

Why do shopping trolleys never go straight?

It's to do with the way that the wheels are attached to the base of the trolley, and it can drive you crazy. All four wheels on a supermarket trolley are casters, which means they can rotate in all directions, and that is what allows the trolley to go all over the place. Also, friction plays a part and if only one of the wheels doesn't run as smoothly as the others then that will make it even more difficult to steer.

What's interesting is that an airport trolley doesn't behave in the same way. This is because airport trolleys have fixed rear wheels and change direction only using the front pair. This makes them much easier to keep in a straight line, so if you were to put fixed rear wheels on your supermarket trolley then your problem would be solved. But airport trolleys are meant for going in straight lines, from baggage to security to check-in etc. In shops, we like to dive one way, then another, sometimes backwards. We are not organised enough to do all our shopping in a straight line, so trolleys with minds of their own are what we have to put up with.

The supermarket trolley was invented in 1937 by Sylvan Goldman, who was an Oklahoma shop owner. Up till then, customers had carried wire baskets, but the invention of the trolley made it easier for them to buy more. Mr Goldman became a very happy and a rich man.

Can you read a bar code upside down?

Bar codes are patterns of vertical black lines with white spaces between, which look like stripes. New codes are being introduced, called 2D codes, and these look more like a chequer board. When a beam of laser light hits the bar code, the light areas reflect the light back to the reader, while the dark areas absorb it. This provides a computer with a long binary number which it can decode to provide the information it requires, such as price and what the goods are. Binary numbers consist only of zero and one, and in the case of a bar code, the white stripe is a zero and the black stripe a one.

So what happens if you pass the bar code in front of a scanner either upside down, or the wrong way? Needless to say, they've thought of that. At the extreme end of each bar code is a 'guard' zone. This contains information which tells the computer if it is reading the right-or left-hand side of the code and so it can flip the information as required.

The first ever supermarket bar code scan took place on 26 June 1974 in a shop in Ohio, USA. It was a 10-pack of Wrigley's Juicy Fruit gum.

How do halogen lamps work?

Conventional light bulbs are filled with an inert gas, like argon. But these bulbs are limited to working at a certain temperature because the tungsten evaporates from the filament and condenses on the cool glass envelope, and eventually the filament breaks down. That's why an ordinary filament bulb can only get so hot before it blows. A halogen bulb enables the filament to run at a higher temperature, so it's much brighter. Halogens are among the most reactive elements known, and there are five of them: fluorine, chlorine, bromine, iodine and astatine.

When the tungsten evaporates from the hot filament of a bulb filled with one of the halogens, often iodine, it forms a vapour which cools as it nears the outer glass. As it cools it reacts with the iodine to form tungsten iodide. The tungsten iodide itself is stable until it comes into contact with the very hot filament, where it breaks down again into its elements, tungsten and iodine. Tungsten is redeposited on the filament and iodine vapour is released to repeat the cycle.

How do they put stripes in toothpaste?

The colours and the white toothpaste are not in separate compartments, and if you really worked hard by kneading the tube near the top, you might be able to mix them all up. First of all, the white toothpaste is injected into the tube, but not to the very top. Extending from the top of the tube, for roughly half a centimetre, is a ring, and it is into this ring that the colours are placed. The ring has outlets around the mouth of the tube. As you squeeze on the tube, white toothpaste is pushed out of the nozzle, but the pressure also forces some of the coloured material from the cylinder through those small outlets at the top. These are deposited as stripes as the toothpaste comes out of the tube.

Why does cling film stop being sticky once it's already been stuck to something?

As you peel cling film from the roll it creates an electric charge. If you then apply it to an insulated body it will be attracted to it. So if you apply the cling film to a piece of cake, it will cling. If you apply it to a cake that is still in a tin, it won't. There has to be a different electrical potential between the film and what you are applying it to. In the case of the cake tin, which is a conductor, the electrical charge, or potential, on the film would dissipate. Cling film can't be re-used because after a while the charge that is created when you pull it from the roll leaks away.

How do Post-It notes work?

They work because of the structure of the glue, which consists of small spheres which only make weak contact with the surface they're pressed onto. Due to the gaps between the spheres, the note itself and the surface being stuck to don't make firm contact because only a few of the spheres are touching the surface at any time. So, the note can easily be removed without damaging either the note or the surface it has been stuck to.

It all started out as a bit of an accident back in the late 1960s. A researcher at 3M came up with a weak adhesive, but couldn't think of anything to do with it. Eventually, someone suggested you could use notes with the glue on as bookmarks, because they were so easily removed. From there it was a small step to the Post-It note and now there can hardly be an office anywhere in the world that doesn't have at least a few examples of this not-very-sticky adhesive around.

When you rip a piece of Sellotape off the roll, why does it sometimes glow?

You may not think you were being all that violent, but when you pull Sellotape off the roll you're also pulling electrons off the atoms. This is no real surprise because it's the electrons in atoms which hold matter together. By pulling matter apart, electrons are sometimes given enough energy to escape their atoms and collect in the neighbouring air. However, these escaping electrons leave the plastic with a positive charge (because you've removed some negatively charged electrons). This imbalance of charges can't last for long and soon the negatively charged electrons fall back to the positively charged atoms. An accelerating electric charge, moving from one level of energy to another, emits light – this is what happens in LEDs (see above). We provide energy by pulling the Sellotape and this energy momentarily frees some electrons which then fall back to where they started. In falling back, the energy which we gave them is converted into light and this light is emitted. That is what you see.

Why do steel ships float?

You wouldn't expect steel ships to float, would you? After all, if you drop a lump of steel in the sea it will sink without trace. But all the world's big ships are made of steel. So what's going on?

There are two reasons things float. Planks of wood, for example, float easily because they have lots of air trapped in their fibrous structures which makes them less dense than water – so they float. But when a steel boat floats it is partly for another reason. There is a very important principle, first discovered by Archimedes. It says that the upward force (of buoyancy) is equal to the weight of water displaced. Suppose a ship weighs

20,000 tons, it will sink into the water until it has displaced 20,000 tons of water. After that it will float.

Also remember that when it comes to floating, it is the average density of the boat that matters, not the density of the steel alone. As a large proportion of a steel ship is air, it will float for the same reason that a plank of wood floats – because it is, on average, less dense than water.

Wooden spoons float, and metal ones sink. Why?

To find out why some materials float and others sink, we have to look at the density of the material. Imagine that you had a really powerful magnifying lens. If you could look very carefully through the lens at the metal spoon you would see a lot of tiny lumps, all packed very closely together. These are the atoms of the metal – they might look a bit fuzzy because they are vibrating, but they aren't going anywhere. You'll also see that the atoms in the metal spoon are very close together and so we say that the metal is a dense material. Now, imagine looking at the air trapped inside a soap bubble. There are atoms in here as well but they are spread out a lot more than the metal atoms were. So we say that the air in the bubble is a lot less dense than the metal.

Now look at the water through the lens. What can we say about the way the atoms in the water are arranged? The atoms in the water are more spread out than the ones in the metal spoon, but they are not as spread out as those in the air inside the bubble. This means that water is less dense than the metal the spoon is made out of, but denser than the air in the bubble. For a material to float on something else, the material that is floating has to be less dense (or the atoms inside it have to be more spread out) than the liquid it is floating on. This means that the bubbles will float, but the metal spoon will sink.

So, what is going on with the wooden spoon? It floats on the water so we can say one thing about it – it must be less dense than the water. But *why* is it less dense? It is a solid, just like the metal, so you might expect the atoms to be very close together and that the wood would be denser than the water and sink. However, wood is unlike metal as it contains a lot of air. Wood is made up of lots of stringy fibres with air-filled gaps in between them. The density of air is much less than water and this means that the overall density of the wood that makes up the spoon is less than that of water and so it floats.

What makes a soap bubble pop?

The pressure inside a soap bubble is greater than the pressure outside by an amount which is four times the surface tension divided by the bubble radius. When a bubble bursts, this difference in pressure tends to split the bubble apart. The process which causes bubbles to pop occurs when there is a small amount of water trapped in the film and this tends to drain to the bottom of the bubble under gravity. Eventually the weight of this region of water becomes too heavy for surface tension to support, and the film begins to split. The difference in pressure makes the split grow and the bubble goes pop. The water drains to the bottom faster in larger bubbles, and this is why large bubbles are less stable.

Why do drops of water on a hot tin tray skim around very quickly?

The temperature of the tin tray needs to be much greater than 100°C for this to happen. At this temperature, any water that comes into contact with the tin will instantly evaporate and this evaporating water forms a cushion of air and water vapour, which the blobs of water can float around on. As they float around, more and more of their water evaporates and replaces the cushion of air that is gradually lost. This in turn creates a large amount of turbulence underneath the blob of water and it is this turbulence that sends it speeding all over the tin tray.

How can you skim a stone across a pond?

In order to skim a stone, it must be spinning and tilted slightly so that its leading edge is a bit higher than its trailing edge. This means the trailing edge will hit the water first. But, because the stone wants to keep spinning along the same axis, the whole stone will jump up – not just the bit that hit the water. And it will keep jumping as long as the stone is spinning.

In effect, the spinning stone is like a gyroscope. Gyroscopes try to keep spinning in the same direction. So rather than tilting over when the stone hits the water, it jumps up to keep its axis pointing in the same direction. You can't skim a round stone because there's no trailing edge to hit the water, and you can't skim a stone that isn't spinning because there's no gyroscope effect to make the stone skip.

The best stones for skimming are flat and palm sized and you should launch the stone between your thumb and forefinger to give it spin. Without spin it won't skim.

Why do magnets only attract certain metals?

Every individual atom is a magnet. However, for a whole object to be magnetic all the individual atoms have to line up in a special way. This can't happen in all materials as their atoms are held too rigidly in place. The atoms in magnetisable materials can move around, so that in the presence of a magnet the atoms align and the material itself becomes magnetic.

Why are flames hot?

When you look at a flame you are watching a very complex process going on. In a fire, oxygen (from the air) is combining very rapidly with a fuel (like wood or coal) and this produces heat, light and a flame. Think of the flame as a sort of test tube inside which the fuel and the oxygen react, producing heat and light and also waste products like carbon dioxide and water (yes, there really is water in a flame). The amount of heat produced when something burns depends upon how well the fuel burns and how much oxygen there is available.

How do safety matches work?

What makes a safety match different from an ordinary match is that safety matches need a special surface on which to strike. The head of a safety match contains sulphur and an oxidising agent (which is a compound that releases oxygen to help fuel a burning process) but together these will not ignite on their own – hence they are safe. But if the head of the match is brought into contact by rubbing against a strip containing phosphorous (which is usually on the strip down the side of the box) then a chemical reaction will take place in which heat is produced, and a flame is produced from the burning of the matchstick itself. If you didn't have the wood, you wouldn't have a match – you'd have a sparkler.

Is there any lead in a lead pencil?

Pencil lead is a mixture of graphite and clay – no lead!

Graphite is one form of the element carbon. Other forms of carbon are diamond – the hardest naturally occurring substance on the Earth, then there's soot, charcoal and coal. Pencils used to be made with lead many years ago, which is how they got their name, but lead is poisonous and so sucking the end of a lead pencil could be quite dangerous. We now use graphite and clay because it is safer, and because we can make pencils of different hardness, so that they are more useful for drawing.

Three candles – one tall, one short and one medium – are set alight and a jar placed over the top of them. The tall one goes out first, then the medium one and finally the small one. Why do the candles go out in this order?

When a candle burns it gives off carbon dioxide. This is a gas that will not support combustion. In other words, if you place a flame into a jar of carbon dioxide it will go out. Carbon dioxide is heavier than air and you would expect it to sink to the bottom of the jar, but because it is hotter, having just been released by the flame, it rises to the top and snuffs out the top candle. This process continues until the middle candle goes out, and finally the lowest candle.

If you balance a candle halfway along its length and light both ends, it will start to rock. What's happening?

If you want to try this then you have to take a candle and expose the wick at both ends. Insert a needle through the candle half way along and balance it between two glasses. Now light both ends. After a while, the candle will move up and down like a see-saw. What is happening here is that the candle is trying to achieve equilibrium – this is a state where all the forces acting on it cancel each other out. As one end burns a little, the candle gives off water and carbon dioxide as the wax melts. So that end of the candle becomes lighter and, like an unbalanced see-saw, it starts to rise. But as it does so, the other end falls. This allows more of the lower flame to come into contact with the wax and so this starts to melt and become lighter. So that end rises. And so it goes on, up and down.

But it's a bit more subtle than that. Newton's third law of motion says that for every action there is an equal and opposite reaction, and so the force of a drop falling from one end of the candle creates an equal upward force which makes the candle tend to rise. Put those two effects together and that's why the candle see-saws.

When is Christmas celebrated at the North Pole?

It's difficult to know when Christmas day starts at the North Pole because it has no official time zones. The Sun doesn't rise above the horizon because it's midwinter, so you can't wait for the sunrise as a signal to raid your stocking. Instead, those at the scientific research bases in the Arctic Circle have defined their own time based on Greenwich Mean Time.

Why is a long screwdriver more powerful than a short one?

It depends exactly what you mean by powerful. The turning force is identical if the handles are the same size. However, the force with which you push the screwdriver into the wall will also affect how well the screwdriver works. The longer screwdriver probably allows for a better position of your body, allowing you to apply both a greater turning force, and more force along the length of the screwdriver forcing the screw into the wall. So it appears as if the longer screwdriver is more powerful, when in fact you are applying more force and that is why it works better.

I heard that humans swallow, on average, three spiders per year whilst sleeping. True or false?

This is one of those tales that everyone thinks is true, but could be completely false – it's called an 'urban myth'. For a start, in order to swallow a spider in your sleep your mouth has to be open. Not everyone sleeps with their mouth open. Spiders tend not to like human beings, so the chances of one being on your bed, let alone near your mouth, are quite small. Also, if you try and blow on a spider it will run a mile so imagine what it would do if it felt your breath.

And although it's true that the swallowing reflex stills works while we sleep (to help get rid of saliva) there's no guarantee that you swallow in response to everything that goes in your mouth – you can stick a nasty-tasting pill in your mouth, but you don't feel the urge to swallow it.

There is a theory that this is a story which was deliberately published to prove how people will believe any old rubbish they read on the Internet!

Why are apples round and not square?

For survival. If apples had corners, they would crack far more easily because the stresses in the skin wouldn't be distributed as evenly as in a sphere. A cracked apple soon goes rotten as the air enters and oxidises the pulp. Somehow, nature has worked out that apples have a better chance of survival if they're the shape of a ball.

If you heat a squash ball, will it bounce higher?

The more flexible a ball is, the higher it will bounce. This is because when the ball hits the floor, kinetic energy is stored in the ball as it is 'squashed' by the impact. This energy can then be released as the ball expands again, sending the ball back up into the air. The more kinetic energy is stored in the downward movement, the more is released as it moves upwards and the higher it goes. Which is another way of saying 'the harder you throw a ball, the higher it will bounce'.

So why does the rubber of the squash ball bounce higher the more you heat it up? Rubber is called an 'elastomer'. This means that it consists of molecules which are coiled up, a bit like springs, and can be stretched out or squashed. The more you heat them up, the more flexible the bonds between the molecules become and the softer the ball becomes, and so the higher it bounces.

Why are the numbers 123 on the top row of a phone, but on a calculator 789 are at the top?

The calculator keypad grew out of the old mechanical calculators that had the '9' placed at the top because of the mechanical way in which these machines were constructed. As technology improved, the layout of the keypad was not changed because everyone had got used to it, even though there was no longer any reason for the '9' to remain at the top.

Telephones, however, were a new invention and underwent many hundreds of tests to make sure that they were as fast, easy and accurate as possible for the user. Trials began in 1962 with the numbers arranged in two rows of five, progressing in 1967 to three rows of three with the zero at the bottom. More trials were conducted and it wasn't until 1976 that the telephone with a keypad became widely available and in the format that we are all used to.

Does a mirror make more light when a light shines on it?

A mirror cannot make more light than there already is in the room. All a mirror does is to bounce what light there is round the room. Normally light is partially absorbed by the surfaces it lands on, so if you were to replace a whole wall of a room with a mirror it might appear brighter because less light was being lost to the wall. If you stand in front of a candle with a mirror behind it, the light emitted by the candle spreads in all directions – some of it towards your eye. But when it hits the mirror, it bounces back, again straight into your eye. So your eye is receiving more light. But no light has been created, it's just that less of it has been lost.

Why is a distant sound louder if the wind is blowing towards you?

There are lots of theories. Here's the simplest. Imagine the flow of air we call the wind is an escalator along which the sound waves have to travel. If the sound is travelling in the same direction as the wind, it needs less energy to make progress and so less of it is lost over distance. When the sound has to travel against the wind, it is fighting it all the time, energy is lost and the level of sound is reduced.

Why does wind dry things?

Things dry out because the water evaporates from the material into the surrounding air. If you have fresh air blowing through the material, then this will be able to take up more moisture than the 'old' air which has been surrounding the wet garment. The 'old' air will be more saturated with water than the 'new' air.

How does wearing several layers of clothes keep you warm?

There are several reasons why wearing lots of clothes can keep you warm, or cold for that matter. Firstly, air is a very good insulator. By trapping air between each layer of clothes, you are creating several layers of insulating material – essentially double-glazing yourself. This can either keep the heat of the sun out, or keep the heat from your body in.

If you want to keep cool, by wearing several layers of clothing you are creating a large temperature difference between the outer layer, which is exposed to the sun, and the inner layer, which isn't. This is especially so if the outer layer is black and absorbs a lot of heat. This temperature difference creates a breeze which cools the body.

Why do you feel cooler when you switch on an electric fan?

Our bodies radiate heat to the surrounding air, causing it to heat up. If there is no breeze this warmer air will, mostly, stay close to the body. When a fan blows room temperature air past the body, it replaces the warmed air with the cooler room temperature air. When the human body is surrounded by warm air, the rate of heat flow from the body into the air slows down because the temperature difference between the body and the air is less than if the air was cool. This means that if the warm air is constantly being replaced by cooler air, then the rate of heat flow from the body will be greater and so the body will be cooler. The room itself will be no cooler when the fan is operating. The air passing over the blades of the fan will not be cooled either, as no heat is being transferred from the air to any part of the fan.

Why do you see rainbow colours in oily water?

Oil is less dense than water and does not mix with it, so it floats on top of the water as a thin film. The oil itself is not rainbow coloured, obviously, so the colouring must be caused by changes in the light reflected off the surface.

When light strikes the surface of oily water, some of it is reflected by the surface of the oil, while some is reflected by the water beneath. The light reflected from the water has travelled further than the light reflected from the oil and this path difference causes something called 'destructive interference'. Interference is where you have two waves (in this case light waves) travelling together at the same time in the same medium. The end result is the net effect of the two waves on the medium through which they travel. This means that sometimes, certain wavelengths of light will be muted and others enhanced. In the case of the film of oil, it will be thicker in some places than others and so the interference will vary. The result is that you see different swirls of colour across the whole film of oil.

Why does a stretched balloon feel warm?

It is because of friction, which inevitably leads to heat. You are putting energy into the material when you stretch it. This causes the molecules in the substance to move apart – in some materials if the stretch isn't too far the energy that is put into the material is returned when the material returns to it normal size. With rubber the molecules are in a jumble, and stretching pulls the polymer structure into long straight lines. On release the elastic slides back to its original shape, but some of the energy which has been supplied is given out as heat when the molecules bang against each other on contraction.

How does an eraser (rubber) manage to remove pencil marks on paper?

Microscopically, paper has lots of bumps and ridges on it and when you write on the paper some graphite from the pencil tip is worn off. This is what leaves the pencil mark on the paper. Graphite sticks very easily to the paper, but it sticks even more easily to vulcanised rubber, which is what erasers are made from. As the eraser is rubbed over the page, every graphite molecule that it comes into contact with makes a better bond with the rubber than with the paper and so the graphite is lifted off the paper. The eraser 'dust' that is left over is simply worn-off eraser with graphite stuck to it. If an eraser is wet, the water molecules lock into the eraser molecules, preventing the graphite from bonding as it would otherwise, and smears your text around rather than rubbing it out.

If a bullet is fired from a gun straight up, is it possible for it to reach its original velocity in its fall back to Earth?

Probably not – not on the Earth anyway. Everything on Earth has a terminal velocity – a maximum speed that can't be beaten. That speed depends on the density of the air the object is moving through. So on the Moon, for example, where there isn't an atmosphere, the bullet would carry on accelerating until it hit the floor. To know for certain whether a bullet reaches its original velocity or not would mean knowing what the original velocity was, and that depends on the type of gun. The only figures we have are that the speed of a bullet ranges from 300 to 500mph. I doubt that a bullet would have a terminal velocity anywhere near this. However, standing under a falling bullet probably isn't wise either!

What is the speed of a bullet in a plane travelling at 1,000mph if the bullet leaves the barrel at 500mph?

It depends who is measuring the speed. If you are standing on Earth and observing the bullet and the plane, then the speed of the bullet when fired forward will be the sum of the two speeds – 1,000mph+500mph=1,500mph. If the bullet is fired at an angle it will have a speed between 500mph and 1,500mph as seen by someone on the ground. But if you were on the plane it would appear that the bullet was travelling at 500mph no matter which direction it was fired in.

Think of it another way. If you walk down the aisle of the plane, to someone on the plane you might be strolling along at 2mph. But someone on Earth, looking up, would see you shooting through the sky at hundreds of miles per hour.

What happens to a ping-pong ball on the surface of a bucket of water in a lift?

Just as bits of your body wobble about in a lift as it speeds its way up and down buildings, so would a ping-pong ball floating on water. As the lift goes up, the ping-pong ball will bob down in the water fractionally and then return to its normal position, and as the lift came to a halt the ball would continue upwards slightly and then return to its starting position. The opposite would happen as the lift went down.

The question is why? It's all to do with 'inertia'. The inertia of the ball is its resistance to a change of velocity. So, if something is stationary it has a certain resistance to any force that tries to make it move. And anything that's moving has a certain resistance to any force that tries to stop it. Because the ping-pong ball isn't physically attached to the lift, when it starts to move the ping-pong ball gets left behind. But because it's floating on water which naturally tries to keep its shape, the ping-pong ball gets pushed back by the water to where it was before.

If a bee is hovering in the inside of a bus at the front, and the bus begins to accelerate to 30mph, will the bee remain at the front of the bus or will it move towards the back?

The real question is what happens to the air inside the bus when the bus begins to accelerate? You don't feel a huge breeze as the air all rushes to the back of the bus, do you? When the bus begins to move off, the air inside the bus also accelerates at the same rate relative to the air outside the window. The bee is hovering relative to the air *inside* the bus, so it will continue to remain where it was in relation to the inside of the bus, and so it will stay at the front of the bus. When the bus starts to move relative to the outside world, the people inside it, the air and the bee, all move together as the bus accelerates.

How do they know how long a bungee jumping rope has to be, so you don't hit the ground?

The key word here is 'elastic', and that doesn't mean the stuff that holds your pants up. In physics, elastic means that a material will stretch when you pull it, then go back to the shape and size it started at when you let go.

Let's try an experiment and do a bungee jump in miniature. Get a long, thin elastic rubber band and hang it from a hook or a door handle – that's your bungee rope. Next, put a weight on the bottom end of the band; a lump of plasticene will do. That lump is you. What's happened? Correct! The rubber band has stretched. It is now longer than when we started, because the weight of the plasticene is pulling down on the end. Now, if you lift the plasticene and then drop it, you will see it goes lower because the band stretches more, then it gets shorter and jerks the plasticene up again. It always stretches the same amount for the same force.

There are three big scientific principles working here. There's 'Hooke's Law', which tells you how much the rope will stretch; then the 'conservation of energy', which says that if you are moving and something stops you, the energy has to go somewhere; and finally the 'conservation of momentum' kicks in as the rope brings you to a halt before it contracts. When you jump off a bridge on a bungee rope, the experts have worked out exactly how much your weight will stretch the rope as you fall. Calculating the length of the rope then requires some quite complex maths; however, they can work out just the right length to make sure that you get very close to the river, the ground, or whatever is under the bridge, but you don't actually hit it.

By the way, bungee jumpers should never lie about their weight!

When a budgie in a cage starts flying, does the total weight of the cage and bird go down?

Amazingly, the total weight would go down. Imagine the cage on a set of weighing scales. When the budgie is sitting on its perch, the total weight is a combination of the weight of the cage and the weight of the bird. When the bird launches itself into space, its weight no longer has any effect on the scales. However, if the bird were to be in an airtight container (and don't try this at home or your budgie might not be too happy) the weight would remain the same. This is because as the budgie flies, it beats its wings and every stroke of its wings pushes a column of air downwards that equals its weight. In a cage with open sides, this air escapes so it has no effect on the weight.

Why do towels dried in a tumble drier come out nice and soft but those dried on a clothes line outside end up hard and rough to the touch?

Try knocking the towel around a bit and you'll see it becomes softer. The towels which have been dried on the line will have dried in one position, and so you end up with a stiff fabric. Those in the tumble drier will have constantly been moving around as they dry so will be soft and supple.

Why does a carpet feel warmer to bare feet than concrete?

The carpet may feel warmer than the concrete but they will all be at the same temperature. So why does the carpet feel warmer? This is to do with how good a conductor of heat the material is. Materials like concrete and metal are very good conductors of heat and when you touch them heat moves from your foot into the material. Because your hand has lost heat, the material feels cool. Materials like carpet are poor conductors of heat – they are said to be insulators. When you touch a carpet, any heat that your hand has stays where it is and so the carpet feels warm.

If water is made of oxygen and hydrogen, why does it put fires out?

Water doesn't burn, because it's already an ash. You are correct that water is made of oxygen and hydrogen, and you are also correct that hydrogen is flammable. However, oxygen is not flammable. Oxygen is an oxidizer; that is, it supports combustion, but a jet of oxygen will *not* burn in air. When oxygen and hydrogen are mixed they can chemically combine, generating lots of heat energy. When this reaction is complete, the product is water. So, water is what is created when hydrogen burns. Water cannot catch fire because one of its constituents has been burnt already.

Why can I see through my window during daylight, but only see a reflection of the interior once it has gone dark?

When you look out of a window during the day, what you can see depends on how much light is available. You see things on the far side of the window because there's lots of light coming through. There's also a lot of light coming from your side of the window, so if someone were to be looking in they'd also be able to see you. But, even during the day, there is always a small amount of light being reflected by the surface of the glass. It's true that glass is essentially transparent, but where there's a change in medium – where the air meets the glass – a small amount of light is reflected back. So, most of the light from outside is getting through to the inside, but a small amount is reflected out; and most of the light from inside is getting through to the outside, but a small amount is reflected back in. During the day we don't notice the bit reflected back to us because it is mostly outshone by the stuff coming through the glass. At night, there is no light from outside to get in so there's nothing to swamp out the reflected light from inside. The reason you can see your reflection is because the incoming light that was blocking it out during the day has been removed.

Why is water wet?

We have to think about what we mean when we say water is wet. Wet means that liquid sticks to things – it sticks to your fingers so they're still covered in water when you pull them out of the sink, and it sticks to clothes so that they're still covered in liquid when we take them out of the washing machine. The question is why does water do this?

The answer is hydrogen bonding. Water (H_2O) is made up of hydrogen and oxygen. The molecules form H_2O, and you will have to imagine the bonds as lines drawn from the oxygen atoms to each of the hydrogen atoms. The oxygen is slightly negatively charged whilst the hydrogen atoms have a slight positive charge. This means the hydrogens are slightly attracted to the nearby oxygen atoms and vice versa. The molecules can also be attracted to anything they're near as long as there's a slight positive or negative charge. So, your hand when it's in the water is attracting the water molecules to it. When you pull your hand out of the water, some of them remain attracted to your hand and pull others with them. Other liquids, like dry cleaning fluid, don't have any hydrogen bonding so the molecules don't stick to anything.

When you have a shower, why does the shower curtain get sucked into the cubicle?

It is called the 'Bernoulli Effect' and it is what makes planes fly. If you have air moving faster on one side of an object than on the other, then that creates a partial vacuum and the object gets sucked to one side. If you take a piece of paper and hold it in front of you face by the corners it will flop down. Blow across the top of it and the paper should lift up. By blowing across the top, you've forced the air to travel faster. That in turn decreases the density of the air so the piece of paper gets sucked upwards.

In a shower, the jet of water creates a downdraft of air that generates a low pressure area behind the curtain. The air in the rest of the bathroom pushes the curtain in and it sticks to your body. If you manage to stick the curtain to the bath before you start, the strength of the hydrogen bonding in the water is usually enough to stop it happening though.

Spaced Out

Shooting stars
to twinkling planets;
cosmic rays to comet tails;
crashing galaxies
to sinking Earth

Does a spirit level work in a spacecraft?

If you were in a place where there was zero gravity, then a spirit level would not work because there would be nothing to make the bubble float one way or another. The bubble would still be there, but its position in the spirit level would have no meaning.

How cold is it in space?

Let's assume we are talking about outer space, which is the bit between the planets, stars and galaxies, and generally reckoned to begin about 60 miles above the surface of the Earth. Out there, space has a temperature of about 3° Kelvin on a temperature scale at which absolute zero is defined as 0° Kelvin. Absolute zero is the temperature at which it becomes so cold that all molecular movement stops, and converts to −273.16°C.

The 3° Kelvin are remnants of the heat from the Big Bang which took place at the very start of the universe. This energy has been spreading out ever since and, although we can no longer see it as visible light, it still exists as background microwave radiation.

How many stars are there in the universe?

If you view the night sky with the naked eye, then the number appears to be around 1,000. But that, of course, is far, far less than the total number of stars out there. Also, you can only see the stars which are visible from your hemisphere. It has been estimated that if you had perfect vision, a perfectly clear sky, and could observe from both hemispheres – none of which could actually happen – you'd see around 9,000 stars. If you add a pair of binoculars, the number jumps to nearly a quarter of a million. But once you move into theory, the numbers grow rapidly. There are more than 170 billion galaxies in the universe, and it's been estimated that in our own galaxy there are around 400 billion stars. So if you do the multiplication the figure you get is, roughly, 10 followed by 24 zeros – a septillion.

What are stars made of?

They are made of very hot gas, mostly hydrogen and helium. The gas gets denser and hotter as you head towards the centre of the star. In the Sun, which is the nearest star to Earth, the temperature reaches 15 million °C. Stars produce other elements in their cores as a byproduct of the nuclear fusion reactions that power them. Most of the material in the Earth, and in our bodies, has been created in this way in the largest stars, and spread throughout the galaxy by supernova explosions.

So are we all made of stars?

In a way, we are, because all the elements that are part of our bodies are found on the stars as well. All the elements we find on Earth, and of which we are made, are the same elements that you will find anywhere in the universe. This is because all elements were created in the same way – at high temperature and under high pressure in the middle of stars.

The simplest atoms, hydrogen and helium, are by far the most abundant in the universe and these were formed during the early life of the universe when it was settling down after the Big Bang. But under the immense temperatures and pressures in the core of the stars, these atoms can fuse together, and this creates a heavier element than the one you started with. This is called nuclear fusion, and when it takes place energy is released, which is why stars shine.

So, all the elements are direct descendants of hydrogen and helium and that is why you will find all the same elements throughout the universe, even on the stars, and within us. So, yes, we are made of stars.

What are shooting stars?

Shooting stars, or 'meteors', are tiny fragments of space rubbish which usually burn up when they hit the Earth's upper atmosphere, leaving only a short bright trail of light behind them.

Many meteors can be predicted. They happen in showers once a year when the Earth crosses a trail of dust and debris left behind by a comet. Meteors can be seen at any time of the year though, and are caused by small particles of left-over material from the birth of the Solar System itself. It's the same material which makes up the asteroids.

Large meteors that hit the Earth are called meteorites. They tend to be the tougher, rather than the flimsy ice balls which comets leave behind. Meteorites fall into three main categories: irons, stones and stony irons. Iron meteorites are almost all metal, made up of 90 per cent iron, 9 per cent nickel, with other elements, and are the most common type found on Earth. Stone meteorites, on the other hand, are very similar to the rocks which make up the Earth's crust itself. They probably outnumber the iron meteorites, but they often blend in with rocks in the landscape. Stony iron meteorites are a cross between the two types. The stony types are often peppered with tiny globules of glassy material, called 'chondrules'.

One other fascinating group of meteorites are those which come from other planets. Since the 1980s, hundreds of fragments of rock have been recovered on the ice planes of the Antarctic – a region where rocks could only be if they had fallen from the sky. Analysis of the rocks has shown similarities with those on the Moon and Mars, so perhaps they were flung off in huge explosions in the distant past, and have rained back onto Earth in the ages since. The fact that these rocks have never been melted suggests that they have been thrown into space by asteroid impacts on the planets, rather than by powerful volcanoes.

When you look at pictures of the Earth taken from space, you never see the stars in the background. Why not?

If you were to take a photo of a candle next to a floodlight lighting up a hockey field, you wouldn't see much of the candle. Cameras aren't like our eyes: they give pictures based on the collection of light for just a split second. Our eyes, or more correctly our brains, compile pictures based on signals from our eyes that might be seconds apart. So we can look at the night sky and the longer we look, the more light we see, not only because more light reaches our eyes but because our eyes and brains become better at making out that light. Even so, we still wouldn't be able to see a candle next to a floodlight. And for the same reason, the bright image of the Earth makes it very difficult to see the dim stars behind. Even the surface of the Moon was too bright for stars to appear in the pictures taken by the Apollo astronauts.

Which star would you have to be on now to see the Earth when the dinosaurs were about?

Dinosaurs lived on the earth over 65 million years ago, so you would need to be on a star further than 65 million light years away. No stars in our galaxy are that far away, so we have to go to another galaxy. Amazingly enough, a galaxy in Virgo called M100 is almost exactly 65 million light years away. Its distance was recently measured by a team in California using data from the Hubble Space Telescope. That's where you should head.

Why don't the constellations change if the stars are moving so fast?

Although the stars are indeed moving very fast (many kilometres each second) they are so far away (typically trillions of kilometres) that they have to travel for thousands of years before we can see a difference in their positions. In one lifetime we won't notice a difference in the constellations, but if you could come back in a few thousand years the sky would look very different. To give an idea of the apparent motion of the most rapidly moving stars, it would take about 200 years for them to move across the diameter of the full moon.

Why don't planets twinkle like stars?

In order for objects in the sky to twinkle, they have to be from a pinpoint source of light. As the light passes through the atmosphere on its way to our eyes, it gets bounced around in the turbulence of the air, and for short periods its light may even be blocked out – that's twinkling. Astronomers call it 'scintillation'.

Because the planets are nearer to us than the stars, they appear in the sky as a disc. This is a much broader source of light, and so it is less likely that light from all parts of the disc would be disrupted in the same way at the same time – so no twinkling. It means that, if you are not certain if an object in the sky is a star or a planet, the twinkling is a good clue. But not always – when a planet is low in the sky, the light has to pass through more atmosphere than when the planet is overhead, so the chances of disturbance to the light are greater. If we had no atmosphere, of course, stars would not twinkle either.

Why is the sky black at night?

This is a question that puzzled people for centuries, only they looked at it the other way round and asked 'why isn't the sky a blaze of light at night if there are stars in all directions?'

The question is known as 'Olbers' Paradox' after the German astronomer, Heinrich Wilhelm Olbers, who popularised the topic in 1823. If the universe had an infinite number of stars, and if the universe were infinitely old, then the light from the limitless number of stars would have had time to reach us and flood the night sky with light. Therefore the universe is not infinite, goes the argument, and that's why the sky is dark. Olbers thought the universe was infinite, but that light from the stars was absorbed by gas and dust in deep space. But there simply is not enough gas and dust in space to make an appreciable difference to light as it travels from distant stars.

So what is the answer? Here's just one explanation. Light has a finite velocity and, put quite simply, the light from the furthest reaches of the universe has not had time to reach us yet, so the universe may indeed be infinite. We shall have to wait and see. It could be a long wait.

Why did the planets in the solar system all travel in the same plane?

The entire solar system was initially formed from a massive ball of gas and dust which slowly started to pull together under the effects of gravity. The centre of the ball got hotter and hotter as dust bumped and stuck together, until it got hot enough to form the Sun. As bits stuck together, the whole thing started spinning because of a law called 'the conservation of angular momentum'. This says that as something gets smaller, it spins faster and faster. For example, as a skater brings their arms into their body and gets smaller, so the skater will speed up. Any slight rotation in the ball of dust and gas that formed in the solar system would have got bigger and bigger as it shrank.

As things spin, forces push the middle out and pull the top in, and this happened with the ball of dust so that eventually it wasn't a ball any longer, but a disc surrounding the Sun. Then, shock waves from nearby supernova created ripples which forced the bits of dust and rock to start to clump together. This in turn encouraged further bits to stick together, and so on.

Is it true that Venus rotates about the Sun in the opposite direction to all the other planets?

No, it's not true. But there is something about the rotation of Venus that makes it unusual. If you were to look down on all the planets in the solar system, you would see that they rotate counter-clockwise – except Venus, which rotates clockwise. This is what astronomers refer to as 'retrograde revolution'. The result is that, on Venus, the Sun would be seen to rise in the west and set in the east.

But why does Venus rotate one way when all the other plants spin the other? To be honest, scientists don't know. But there are plenty of theories. The latest says that Venus originally spun the same way as all the others until something caused it to flip over on its axis so that it was, sort of, upside down. The planet would, of course, continue to spin in the same direction but because it was upside down it would appear to us as though it was spinning the wrong way. The next question must be what might have caused Venus to flip? We don't know the answer to that either.

Why is the Earth or any large astronomical object round?

Large astronomical bodies are (almost) round because of gravity. Stars and planets which aren't solid are pulled towards the centre of the body evenly in all directions. If you pull something in all directions, you end up with a sphere. Any bit that tries to stick out gets pulled back in by gravity. When the solar system was formed, the planets were fairly molten until they cooled down. During this time, gravity was able to pull them together into a sphere.

Is the Sun round?

The Sun isn't exactly round – it's what's known as an 'oblate spheroid', which is a sphere which has been squashed slightly, so it's fatter than it is tall. If you sit on a roundabout and start to spin, you will feel a force trying to throw you out from the centre. This is called a 'centrifugal' force. The same thing is happening in the Sun. It's spinning so quickly that all its mass is being thrown outwards. Because of the Sun's gravity, this matter can't escape entirely so it's heaped up around the equator – the furthest point from the axis of the Sun, making it look squashed. It's not just the Sun that's squashed though. None of the planets in the solar system are completely spherical. Even the Earth gets squashed because it's spinning – even though it's made of rock.

Why don't we get dizzy because the world goes round?

When we stand on the surface of the Earth, we can't really tell that it's spinning because everything on the Earth is spinning at the same speed. Imagine you're in a car travelling along a nice smooth piece of road. If you shut your eyes you can't really tell you're moving. You only know you're moving when you look at the scenery around you because everything in the car is moving at the same speed. The same is true for the Earth. We can only tell we're spinning when we look at the Sun or the stars moving across the sky. This is how dizziness works: it's actually your ears that makes you dizzy. Inside your head, in part of your ear, are 'canals' filled with a liquid. As you move about, that liquid sloshes around too. When you spin round really quickly, the liquid in your ear starts to spin around. When you stop spinning, the liquid keeps on spinning as it always takes a bit of time for liquid to slow down. So your ears are telling you you're still moving, whilst your eyes are telling you that you're not. Your brain gets confused and you get dizzy.

When the Earth spins, the liquid in your ear doesn't move because you're moving at the same speed as the Earth, and so the liquid in your ears is as well. Everything is moving at the same speed so your brain doesn't get confused.

How far is it to space?

Officially, people who have been to an altitude of more than 80km are classed as astronauts, but only because it seems a convenient number. There is no real dividing line between our atmosphere and space because it gradually thins out. Up to about 80km altitude, the composition of the atmosphere is about the same as it is on the Earth's surface, i.e. 78 per cent nitrogen and 21 per cent oxygen, although the density of the air gets very much thinner with increasing altitude. Above this height, the chemical composition changes and above about 2,000km the atmosphere is mainly hydrogen.

It's an interesting thought that if you could drive a car vertically through the air, you'd be in space in less than an hour.

How long would it take a bus to get to the Sun?

Let's say the bus is travelling at about 30mph and it doesn't stop for anyone. The Sun is 93 million miles away, so the bus would take 3,100,000 hours; or 129,167 days; or 353 years, 321 days and 16 hours.

If the bus broke down and you were walking to the Sun, how long would it take?

The distance to the Sun is 93.5 million miles (149.6 million km). If you walk about 4 miles every hour (which is fairly brisk) it would take you 23.4 million hours, which is 974,000 days or 2,670 years, to reach the Sun. If a new generation occurs every twenty years and you are allowed five years to grow before you start walking, then it would take 107 generations to reach the Sun.

Where does the solar system end?

The solar system stretches out far beyond the orbits of the planets we can see. It stretches to a point around two light years from the Sun, called the 'heliopause', where the Sun's influence finally gives way to interstellar space. The outer solar system is only now being discovered using space telescopes, and a new generation of Earth-based telescopes are starting to identify small asteroids in the space beyond Pluto. These objects are generally smaller than Pluto, and are believed to form a ring around the solar system called the Kuiper Belt.

Beyond lie the Oort Clouds which are two vast shells that surround the solar system. These are made up of debris left over after the solar system's formation, and this is the region where the majority of comets are thought to originate. The outer cloud extends to 1.5 light years from the Sun (the Earth is 8 light minutes from the Sun, and Pluto never goes further out in its orbit than 5.5 light hours). At this distance, the Sun's gravitational influence is weak and collisions between comets can send them spiralling into the warmer regions near the planets; but passing stars can just as easily pull them away from the solar system.

Beyond the Oort Clouds, the solar system is only marked by the influence of the solar wind from the Sun. At around 2 light years out, this is overwhelmed by the stellar winds of billions of other suns. We do not know whether this boundary is marked by a shockwave, or if the solar system gently merges with interstellar space.

Why does Saturn have rings?

First of all, it's not just Saturn that has rings: Jupiter, Uranus and Neptune also have them. However, these rings are very small and faint and so can't be seen from the Earth, and they were actually discovered by the space crafts, Voyager One and Two in the mid-1980s. The fact that all the gas giants (as the outer planets made of gas are known) have rings suggests to astronomers that whatever caused them in the case of Saturn, also caused them around the other planets.

There are two possible theories as to how they formed. The first says that the rings are made up of rock and dust that was formed by asteroids colliding near to the planet. The gravity of Saturn and its moons has since trapped the dust and rocks into the rings we see today. The second theory goes like this: when the planets were forming from the dust and gas cloud, not all the dust and gas was collected by the planet. In other words, the rings are simply stuff left over from when the planets formed. Now if astronomers could find out how old the rocks in the rings were, they might be able to tell which theory was right.

A lot of people think the first theory is right because Jupiter, Uranus and Neptune have such faint rings. They say Saturn's rings are only bright because they were formed 'recently' – which in astronomical terms means millions of year ago – from asteroids colliding. The other planets' rings aren't as bright because they formed a long time ago and most of the bits in the rings have been sucked into the planet.

Why can't we fly planes into space?

One day in the near future we may be able to. Developing a workable 'spaceplane' would make it easier and cheaper to fly around the world or reach orbit, and would be a major step towards opening up space for everybody. But it's no good simply modifying existing aircraft designs, because the entire principle of a modern aircraft relies on a reasonably thick atmosphere. All powerful modern planes use jet engines which suck air in through a giant spinning fan called a turbine, then burn it with aircraft fuel to produce a hot and compressed exhaust, and then push this out through the back of the engine. The exhaust gases escape at such high speeds that they push the plane forwards, effectively pushing against the air around the plane. When the atmosphere becomes thin, as it does quite rapidly as we leave Earth, the jet principle becomes less efficient. Also, a jet engine is quite weak compared to a rocket engine and a plane is kept in the air by the design of its wings, rather than the thrust of the jets.

But rockets also have disadvantages. They have to be built from scratch for each new launch, and there is the added expense of special fuels, launch sites and technology. Something that combines the best aspects of rockets and normal aircraft would be the best of both worlds; then it could take off and land from normal airports, and fly like a plane in the atmosphere and like a rocket in space. It could also return to Earth in one piece and ready to be refuelled and launched again.

If it takes light so long to get from the edges of the galaxy, how do we know what's going on there today?

We don't! You're right to suggest that light from a galaxy that is a million years old only tells us that the galaxy was there a million years ago. It might not be there now. But astronomers are used to working in the past. In a sense they are like geologists – always digging into the past.

Unfortunately, we tend to forget to mention this to people when we tell them what we've found. So, a news report might say 'Astronomers have found a new galaxy at the edge of the universe'. That's ambiguous for a number of reasons. First of all there isn't really an edge to the universe; it's more an edge to the observable universe. In other words, the edge is only as far as we can see. Secondly, it's ambiguous because the galaxy isn't new – it's old; we just see it as being new. The news will often mention that the light from distant objects has taken thousands or millions of years to reach us, and might say the light left when dinosaurs were still roaming the Earth.

As far as the 'edge' of the universe is concerned, there isn't one. If you head off in one direction and keep going you'll come back to where you started. The universe is a hypersphere – a four-dimensional sphere. Think of it as an onion. The universe is the outer layer of the onion. We can't see this layer; we can only see the inner layers. The further we look, the further back in time we're looking, and the further into the onion we go. Astronomers have learnt to live with the fact that they can only work in the past, but they don't mind because it gives them an insight into how the universe and the galaxies within the universe were formed.

Where do cosmic rays come from, and are they hitting us all the time?

Cosmic rays are charged particles with very high energies (so not rays at all) that enter the Earth's atmosphere, and they are doing so all the time. It's thought that cosmic radiation is energy left over from the Big Bang. Cosmic rays consist mainly of protons, together with electrons and nuclei. In outer space their paths are guided by the magnetic field lines of the Earth and Sun, and in the space of just several minutes a few hundred cosmic rays will have passed through your body. But we don't think that's too much of a problem – the magnetic field around the Earth acts as a shield, called the magnetosphere. However, cosmic rays can become a problem for pilots of high-flying aircraft, and certainly astronauts.

There is, of course, one kind of cosmic radiation which is harmful and that is UV radiation, which burns our skin and can raise the risk of skin cancer.

Why doesn't the Sun go out in space where there's no oxygen?

It's true that burning is usually fuelled by oxygen, but that is not the case with the Sun. In the Sun, the heat and light comes from a different sort of reaction called nuclear fusion. Here the inner bits of atoms (the nuclei) collide and fuse together. Each fusion reaction releases a million times as much energy as a single chemical reaction – that is how the Sun can burn so brightly and for so long (about 10 billion years). This reaction does not need oxygen, so it does not matter that there is not any oxygen in space.

Why do the tails of comets appear to be curved?

The tail of a comet can be several million kilometres long, and is made up of very small dust particles around the size found in cigarette smoke. These have been released from the comet's nucleus. The comet itself consists of lumps of ice, dust and gases. The small particles in the tail, once released, then try to take up an orbit round the Sun. The end result is that the particles making up the tail are made up of different particles on different orbits around the Sun, all somewhat similar to that of the comet, but the small differences are enough to give the characteristic curved shape.

All comet tails point away from the Sun due to the solar wind, which is an invisible stream of matter and radiation escaping from the Sun.

What is the danger of a comet or asteroid hitting the Earth?

In the long term, it's an absolute certainty. Every few months, we seem to be reminded of the danger, as another asteroid sweeps past the Earth at *only* a few million kilometres – which is a cosmic hair's breadth.

A small body of about 2km striking the Earth would cause a crater 30km in diameter – that's the size of London. A major problem would be the amount of dust thrown up from such an impact. This would darken the sky and reduce the amount of energy and light from the Sun getting to the surface, causing the planet to cool.

The Earth is already covered with the signs of past impacts. We now know for certain that a large object hit Earth at the same time as the dinosaurs were wiped out, and that this was only one of many. As recently as 1908, something (probably a comet fragment) crashed into Siberia at Tunguska, wiping out 2,000 square kilometres of forest, and only missing Moscow by two hours.

In the shorter term, though, we really don't know when the next impact will occur. All we can hope is that it won't happen in our lifetimes. There's always a chance of a comet appearing from the outer solar system on a collision course and often they are only discovered as they rush past us in a 'near miss'! Scientists have developed 'Project Spaceguard', which is a plan to map the orbits of every substantial object in an Earth-crossing orbit. With a network of powerful telescopes dedicated to the search, they predict Spaceguard could increase the discovery rate of these objects to several thousand per year.

If an approaching impact was discovered in time, then with today's technology it might be possible to prevent it. The amount of warning we have is crucial. If an approaching object was discovered only days or weeks before impact, there would be little to do but take cover and hope. With a warning of a few months or longer, preparations could be made to intercept the object. An obvious way of dealing with the threat would be to destroy the object with a rocket-delivered nuclear bomb. However, such an explosion could multiply the problem, creating a swarm of smaller planetoids on course for Earth. A far better solution is to divert the asteroid, which could be done in one of two ways. A small nuclear bomb could be landed on one side of it and then detonated; or alternatively a powerful rocket engine could be anchored to the surface of the asteroid, pushing it slowly into a different course over a long period.

Is it always full Moon everywhere on the Earth?

Yes, it is. The phases of the Moon are caused by the relative positions of the Sun and Moon as viewed from the Earth, so no matter where you are on the Earth, you will see the same Moon. At full Moon, the Sun, Moon and Earth fall along the same line. You might think the Earth would cast a shadow on the Moon, but their orbits are not in exactly the same plane so the Earth usually passes above or below the shadow. When they coincide, that is when you get an eclipse.

What happens to plants in weightless conditions?

With no gravity to determine which direction the roots grow in, plants have to rely on other factors. In general, the shoots will just keep on growing in the direction the seed was planted, and the main root will head off in the other direction at the same time, being sensitive to the direction that light and moisture is coming from.

Where do the bubbles in fizzy drinks go in zero gravity?

On Earth, there is an upwards force on the bubble because, thanks to gravity acting on the liquid, the pressure is slightly greater at the bottom of the bottle than at the top. If you are in something like a space shuttle, gravity is still acting but it is compensated for by the acceleration in the (circular) orbit – which is why things appear weightless in space. The same happens to bubbles. They would just hang around in the liquid and gradually join to form larger bubbles.

What actually happened during the Big Bang?

According to the Big Bang theory of the creation of the universe, everything was created around 10 billion years ago in a single massive explosion. The Big Bang model really shows what happened after the explosion, but is vague about the explosion itself. Cosmologists say that space and time themselves were created in the explosion, so there's no point in asking what happened 'before', because there was no 'before'. They also say that, up till 1×10^{35} seconds (0.000[for 31 more 0s]1 seconds) after the Big Bang, the universe was so small that it didn't obey the normal laws of physics. From then on, though, the Big Bang theory does a good job of describing how the universe got to be like it is today.

The creation of the universe divides up into several distinct periods of time, or eras. Firstly, the 'Particle Era': as the universe emerged from the Big Bang, it's temperature was incredibly high, so high that energy could convert into particles of matter such as the protons, neutrons and electrons which make up atoms of the everyday material around us. As the universe expanded near the speed of light, the energy became much more thinly spread and the temperature rapidly dropped, until after one second it had fallen to 10 billion degrees Celsius. At this point there was not enough energy to create more matter – everything we see in the universe today had already been created in a raw state. Remember, we're only one second after the Big Bang at this stage.

Then came 'nucleosynthesis': as the temperature continued to drop, it eventually reached a point at which stable groups of protons and neutrons were able to form and stay together. These combined to form the central nuclei of hydrogen and helium atoms, the simplest elements in the universe. This is why the universe is still dominated by hydrogen and helium today.

Then followed the 'Radiation Era' and even if we could look far back in time we wouldn't be able to see any evidence of this because the universe was so dense that the light was trapped inside the expanding universe and much of the universe's energy was now in the form of radiation.

Finally came the 'Matter Era'. The radiation era lasted to around one million years after the Big Bang and continued for 200 million years, and as the universe's temperature dropped off, it eventually reached 3,000 degrees Celsius, the temperature at which stable hydrogen atoms are able to form. The atomic nuclei began to absorb the electrons that were floating around among them, forming stable atoms, and clearing the universe to a point where eventually most of its energy was bound up in matter, which was now so widely spread that light was finally able to rush off in all directions towards the edge of the universe. This is when the stars and galaxies formed.

Why is the universe expanding?

Well, most people now accept the idea of the Big Bang – an initial 'explosion' of matter, time and space from a single point, what scientists call a singularity. This explosion created everything in the universe – including the space between matter, and time itself. Expansion is the natural result of any explosion as particles are thrown away from each other. In a sense, this is what's happening to the universe except that it's not really the matter that's expanding, it's the space.

How do we know the universe is expanding?

We know the universe is expanding because of the work of the astronomer Edwin Hubble in the twentieth century. He thought that since there was nothing special about our own place in the universe, if he were to observe the distant stars and galaxies he would find that some are moving away from us, and some getting closer in a random kind of way. But what he found was that *all* the galaxies were moving away from us. It also fits in with the general relativity theory of Albert Einstein who predicted this would happen.

But how did Hubble work out in which direction the galaxies were moving? What he observed is what is called 'red shift'. In other words, the light emitted by these distant galaxies was shifted towards the red end of the spectrum. This, he realised, was the 'Doppler effect' and occurs when a source of waves (light or sound) moves towards or away from the observer, and a change in frequency is observed. You will probably have experienced this for yourself – if a police siren moves towards you, and then quickly passes you, the note seems to drop. Hubble worked out that for the red shift to occur, it must mean the source of the light was moving away from us, and so by measuring the shift he could work out the speed.

Is there anybody out there?

If you mean intelligent life, then unfortunately there's no evidence for it so far. There are certainly some unexplained UFOs or Unidentified Flying Objects, but if aliens are really trying to contact us, why don't they drop in and see us? Any astronomer would have to be very brave, though, to say that the Earth was the only life-bearing planet in the universe, because there are plenty of people who'd say that intelligent life is thinly-scattered in our own galaxy.

So, what are the essentials for the formation of life in other places? For a start, life would need a long period of stability to develop in the first place, and even longer to evolve beyond microbes into complex animals and plants. Evolution is a very slow process, and there's no reason to think it would go any quicker on other planets. So, the first requirement would have to be a stable sun. This immediately rules out 90 per cent of the galaxy's 200 billion stars because they are either too cold and feeble, or too hot and short-lived. Any star which might have life on its planets would need to be very much like our own. Another essential is the presence of water. In order to form complex molecules, chemicals need to be able to mix together well, which is something they can't do as solids or gases. Water is especially good at dissolving chemicals to form solutions. Although water molecules are widespread throughout the universe, water is only

liquid in a narrow range of temperatures and pressures, so for liquid water to survive on a planet, it would need a substantial atmosphere and a stable orbit around its star at roughly the same distance as the Earth. Even these two simple requirements rule out any of the other solar systems we know about.

The discovery of planets round other stars at least makes life elsewhere in the galaxy a little more likely. But even if a planet was able to evolve life, it would still have to overcome a lot of hurdles to reach our level. For example, the lucky presence of Jupiter in the outer solar system has taken comet impacts which might have wiped us out, and therefore reduced the occurrence of mass-extinctions like the one which may have killed the dinosaurs. We have been allowed time to develop at our own pace and, in several hundred million years of history, to develop the use of tools, technology and civilisation.

Of course, we are only talking about the kind of 'life' we know and understand. There may be other forms of 'life' that we cannot even imagine.

What's at the centre of our galaxy?

The problem is that we can't get a good look at the centre of the galaxy because of all the dust clouds in the way. The Sun is a third of the way towards the edge of the galaxy, and the stars become much more tightly packed towards the centre – roughly half the galaxy's stars are packed into a cluster 30,000 light years across. This is why the Milky Way is much brighter in the direction of the constellation Sagittarius, which is where the nucleus lies.

So, the nucleus is basically a huge ball of stars. But what lies at the centre, and what pulled them all together in the first place? We know that the galaxy rotates more slowly at greater distances from the nucleus, and so the nucleus is spinning relatively quickly. Astronomers believe that the centre of the nucleus must contain around one million solar masses of material in a region only a couple of light years across. By looking at the nuclei of other galaxies, and studying the radio signals, we know that something very violent must be happening there.

The two favourite theories at the moment are that the core of the galaxy contains an extremely compacted star cluster, where the gravitational interplay of the stars could generate tremendous amount of energy, or that all the mass is contained in a single huge black hole, which is a collapsed region of space with gravity so strong that not even light can escape. This black hole could consume material from the surrounding nucleus. As the matter is sucked in, it would be heated to extreme temperatures, giving off large amounts of radiation before being destroyed. Fortunately, even if the black hole theory is correct, its influence is confined to within a few light years of the centre of the galaxy.

Do galaxies collide?

Yes, it's how galaxies grow and evolve. At present about 10 per cent of galaxies are interacting with another, and over time they all do so. Dramatic collisions of two equal-size large galaxies are most spectacular, and rare, but galaxies only get bigger by eating their neighbours. Interestingly, the galaxy currently being eaten up by the Milky Way was discovered only ten years ago.

Why doesn't the Earth sink in space?

In a way, the Earth is sinking in space towards the Sun, although 'falling' might be a better word to use. The Earth is pulled towards the Sun all the time by gravity. If we weren't moving around the Sun quickly enough, we'd fall towards it in a matter of moments. But I guess your question really asks, why doesn't the Earth fall downwards through space? If you live in the northern hemisphere, then you automatically think of down as being south. So, why doesn't the Earth fall southwards through space? Well firstly, who's to say which way is down? We think down is southwards, but that's only because all the maps we see have us at the top. If Australia was always at the top, we'd think north was down. But the real reason why the Earth doesn't fall north or south is because there's nothing there to pull it that way. The only big pull on the Earth is from the Sun.

Why doesn't gravity make satellites fall from the sky?

If the satellite were stationary, it would fall straight back down to Earth. In fact, satellites are falling towards the Earth all the time, but the Earth keeps getting out of the way.

There are two forces at work on a satellite; the first is the gravitational force of the Earth, which draws the satellite towards the centre of our planet. The other force is provided by the motion of the satellite and is called the 'centrifugal force'. If one is greater than the other, the satellite either crashes to Earth or flies off into space; but if the forces balance, the satellite stays in orbit. In the end, all satellites will fall back to Earth as their velocity decreases, but in some cases this can take hundreds if not thousands of years. There's no danger of them raining down on your head, though, because they will burn up on entry into the atmosphere and all you might see is something in the sky that looks like a shooting star.

What is dark matter?

From what we can see, the galaxies aren't moving around as they should. We've done all the mathematics and somehow it doesn't come out right – the galaxies simply don't behave. So we've invented this stuff called 'dark matter' which exists out there in the universe, which we can't see, which doesn't absorb or emit light or any other kind of radiation, but has a gravitational effect on the movements of galaxies. Whether it exists, or not, is a different matter. In other words – we've made it up to explain what we have observed.

When will the Sun go out?

The Sun was born about 5,000 million years ago and we can predict that it has enough hydrogen to continue much as it is for another 5,000 million years, then it will begin to swell. As the Sun turns into a red giant it will swallow up Mercury, and then Venus. The Sun, as it started to go out, would look very big and very red. This bloated Sun would boil away the Earth's oceans, destroying any life that has not fled to another planetary system. Then the Sun would engulf the Earth itself. Eventually, the Sun's outer layers will puff away as a beautiful planetary nebula, leaving a white dwarf at the centre of the solar system, circled by the charred remnants of its remaining planets.

If we are looking for somewhere to run to, Mars is probably the closest alternative to Earth, although there is an issue with temperature, but by that stage we must have developed some sort of climate and atmospheric control anyway, and if the Sun was going out it might be the least of our problems.

What happens if you go into space without a space suit?

In outer space without a protective suit, a human being would asphyxiate as there is no air to breathe. Your body would slowly freeze if it fell into the shadow of a larger body, or your blood would boil if you went too close to the Sun. What a space suit is trying to do is create around you the same atmosphere you would experience on Earth. It provides pressurised air (although much lower than the air pressure on Earth) and this prevents the fluids in your body from boiling – remember, there is a relationship between the boiling points of liquid and the air pressure. Because the air pressure is lower, the space suit needs to feed you more oxygen and also regulate your temperature to stop you from roasting in the full Sun, or freezing to death when the Sun is not visible.

The other vital job a space suit does is to protect you from attack by micrometeoroids, which are tiny fragments of rocks which have broken away from larger chunks and are plentiful in space.

Food for Thought

Bubbling water
to tasty burgers;
smelly cheese to stinking eggs;
cracking ice to flaming brandy

What makes the sizzling sound when you put food into a hot pan?

Imagine you've just dropped a slice of bacon into a frying pan. As it heats up, the fat starts to melt and collects in the pan. At the same time water is also released from the bacon but, as the two can't mix, and as both are rather hot, they end up trying to get out of each other's way and they do it rather violently. This rapid movement is the noise that you can hear.

Why does water bubble when it boils?

As water is heated, its molecules become more excited as they gain extra heat energy and this causes them to move around more. At a certain temperature, some of the molecules of water have enough energy to change into a gas and become water vapour. This can happen within the body of water and so bubbles of water vapour form. This water vapour is less dense than the water itself, so it rises and as it does so it expands until it escapes the water's surface, the bubbles burst, and the vapour appears as steam.

Why does toast taste different to bread?

When you toast bread two things happen to it. Firstly, as a result of the heat, the water in the bread evaporates, which dries out the bread. Then, sugars on the surface of the bread begin to caramelise, which means they turn brown and develop a nutty or caramel flavour. These reactions result in the bread turning brown. Caramelisation is the name given to the extensive chemical reactions that occur when any sugar is heated to the point when it begins to break apart. More than a hundred different compounds, many of which have distinct flavours, are made during caramelisation. The chemical reactions which occur during toasting also occur when you make caramel sweets, which probably explains why toast and toffee are so popular.

Which type of milk goes sour first?

Take skimmed milk first. It's a byproduct of cream manufacture. Once the cream is removed from the full-fat milk, what is left over is bottled as skimmed milk. By this time the skimmed milk is already two days old, so the freshest milk is full fat as it is processed the fastest. Skimmed and semi-skimmed milk often don't keep as long due to the longer processing time. That's one theory anyway, and would suggest that full fat milk lasts the longest.

Here's another. It's the action of bacteria that causes milk to go off. They do this by releasing enzymes which break down the milk. One of these is called protease and it is the byproduct of protease that gives sour milk its bitter taste. It's thought that the greater number of fat globules in whole milk prevents some of the action of the protease, and so the milk lasts longer.

What makes chillies hot?

The chemical component of peppers which makes them hot is the alkaloid 'capsaicin' and they have no fewer than five effects on your mouth. Three of them give quick sensations in the back of the palate and throat, and the other two give a long, low sensation on the tongue and mid-palate. In other words, one hits you quick and the other takes its time. How much a pepper will burn you is due to differences in the proportions of these five.

Capsaicin is a general irritant and so can burn skin that is already damaged by cuts or abrasions, and not just on your mouth and throat. The body's response to capsaicin is a defensive one and the result is pain, watery eyes and a runny nose, and a quick dash for a glass of water, or full cream milk which is also said to be a cure for chilli burn. Capsaicin dissolves more easily in fats and oils than it does in water, which is why the milk may be a better treatment. Yogurt works well too.

When salt dissolves in water, does the water volume become greater or does adding the salt make no difference?

If you were to add 5g of salt to 20g of water, stir it in, then weigh it, you would find the total to be 25g. The salt does not disappear, but it has its crystal structure pulled apart when it dissolves in the water. So you have all your water molecules, plus salt molecules, floating around in the same glass. Notice I say *plus* salt molecules. That means you have more molecules than just the water alone. More molecules will take up a greater volume even though it may not be visible to the eye.

If I put a cup of sugar into a cup of water and stir till the sugar has dissolved, I don't end up with two cupfuls of liquid. Where's the sugar gone?

What's happened is that the sugar has filled the spaces between the water molecules by breaking the bonds which hold the water molecules together. What you see when you look at a grain of sugar is really a large collection of molecules, and once the sugar is dropped in the water they are able to split apart and spread throughout the liquid. That's why the sugar looks as though it has disappeared. As far as the volume is concerned when a solid is added to a liquid there will always be a reduction in the net volume. If the solid dissolves in the liquid there may be a further reduction in volume as the solid particles interact with the liquid, drawing it closer.

Why does the sugar dissolve faster if the water is hot?

The higher the temperature of the liquid, the greater the motion of the molecules. Some of this energy transfers to the sugar molecules as they are added to the water and allows the sugar to break apart the liquid molecules faster.

Why does it take our bodies less time to burn things like sugars than it does to burn protein?

There are two reasons. Firstly, the body can only use one type of molecule as a source of energy and that molecule is sugar, or glucose. When you eat carbohydrates, like bread, which are just long chains of sugars bound together, it is very easy for your body to break the bonds between those sugars and then use those sugars for energy. When you eat protein or fats, however, it takes longer because the body has to convert the protein and fat molecules into glucose before it can use them. The second reason has to do with where the foods are actually digested. Sugars and carbohydrates are digested by enzymes in saliva but protein and fats are not digested until the stomach and intestines.

Why do burgers taste so good?

It's probably the fat that gives you the thrill when you eat a burger. Fats are a hugely popular element of food because of their various flavours, their smooth texture, and the feeling of fullness they produce when you eat them. Fats dissolve in the warmth of your mouth and on your tongue, and release some of their fat flavours into the food. Without a little fat, these flavours would remain locked in and the food would be far less tasty. Besides releasing flavours, fat also holds the flavours in the mouth for longer. You can have an intense water-soluble flavour, but it is gone almost instantly. With a fat-soluble flavour, the fat coats the inside of the mouth, holding the flavour there longer for you to enjoy.

Why does Marmite go pale when you tap it?

If you don't believe it, try it for yourself. Put some Marmite on a plate and tap it with your knife (for quite a long time) and it will start to go white. What is happening is that by hitting it you are trapping lots of small bubbles of air in it; you are basically turning it into a foam. The colour change occurs because of the way that these air bubbles reflect the light that hits the Marmite. Normally, Marmite is brown because all wavelengths of light, except those that make brown light, are absorbed by the Marmite. The brown light is reflected and so we see Marmite as brown.

Once the air bubbles have been introduced, the range of light reflected is changed. As more bubbles are introduced, more wavelengths of light will be reflected until almost all of the light hitting the Marmite is reflected and it appears almost white. The air bubbles only stay within the Marmite for a few days, and as they burst the Marmite slowly returns to its original dark brown colour.

Why do humans cook meat but lions and tigers don't have to?

Animals in the wild eat raw meat all the time and have been doing so for thousands of years. Humans *can* eat raw meat, and in some places this is considered a great delicacy, but we will usually cook our meat for two main reasons: the first is that we prefer the taste of it that way, simple as that.

The other important reason we cook meat is to protect ourselves. Animals will usually eat meat fresh, or within a few days of the kill, so they don't have to transport it around and deliver it to shops and restaurants like we do. This time factor is very important when it comes to contamination. Humans have a very poor tolerance to the many micro-organisms which can be found in meat and we can become very ill. The older the meat is, the more of these dangerous micro-organisms are likely to be present. Cooking the meat will destroy almost all of the bacteria and viruses which can make us sick. Animals, on the other hand, have built up a far better tolerance to such contamination. Domestic animals such as dogs and cats come somewhere in between us and their wild relatives, and have slightly different ways of dealing with foods. Cats protect themselves by being very careful feeders; their phenomenal sense of smell will warn them if their food is at all 'off' and they will simply not eat it. Dogs are scavengers, and will eat pretty much anything as their digestive system is incredibly tough and can cope with almost anything.

Why does cheese smell bad?

Not all cheeses smell bad. Think of toasted cheese, for example – that smells wonderful. But it's true that some cheeses smell so foul that you have to be brave to open the fridge door.

It's all to do with the way cheeses are made. They all start out life as milk to which special bacteria are added. This causes the milk to curdle, and it separates into curds and whey. Curds are solid, white lumps, and whey is a watery, cloudy liquid. It is the

curds which eventually make the cheese. Different cheeses use different bacteria to start off the process and this is the key to the cheesy smell. Some bacteria give the eventual cheese a foul smell, others may leave hardly any smell at all. The most famous stinky cheese ever is said to be Limburger. When it's fresh it's quite harmless, but after a couple of months it starts to get really high as the fermentation starts to fully kick in. They say that to compare it to smelly feet is unfair to smelly feet. However, it *is* a fair comparison, because the bacteria used to make the cheese are called *brevibacterium linens*, which are exactly the same bacteria that make body odour!

Is it true that bananas give off gas?

Bananas give off gas as they ripen, and that gas is called 'ethylene'. It is found in other fruits apart from bananas; it's also found in apples, tomatoes and pears. It plays a part not only in ripening, but in the processes which cause plants to open their flowers (for fertilisation), and also to shed leaves. It's harmless to humans. Certain fruits and vegetables are more sensitive to ethylene than others, and if you store them close to ripening bananas you will find that they start to ripen quickly, then go off. Cucumbers can turn to mush and carrots become bitter. If you have a fruit bowl in your kitchen, it might be a good idea to keep the bananas elsewhere.

How do you stop an egg from cracking when you boil it?

The shell of an egg is not as solid as it looks, and is covered with between 7,000 and 17,000 tiny pores all over the shell surface. As the egg ages, moisture and carbon dioxide diffuse out, and air diffuses in, causing the air cell inside the egg to grow. The shell is covered with a protective coating called the 'cuticle'. By blocking the pores, the cuticle helps to preserve freshness and prevent microbial contamination of the contents, which is why eggs should not be washed before they are to be used. If you want to stop an egg from cracking when you boil it, you must add a few drops of vinegar to the water. Vinegar is acidic, and binds with egg whites to make them firmer so, in the pan, a little of the acidic mixture will enter the egg through the pores and create a very thin but firm layer just inside the shell. This means that if the shell should crack, the white won't leak out. Incidentally, because the egg shell is made of calcium carbonate, if you leave an egg long enough in vinegar (acetic acid) the shell will dissolve.

Why do cooked eggs smell so bad?

The reason for this lies with the basic chemistry of an egg. The albumen, or white of an egg, contains a fair amount of sulphur. When this protein is heated, some of the sulphur atoms will be set free and become able to react with hydrogen ions in the albumen. This forms the gas, hydrogen sulphide, which is the smell we associate with rotting eggs. Just because you can smell it, though, doesn't mean that the egg is old or there's anything wrong with it. It's simply because it's been cooked.

Why do bad eggs float?

As soon as an egg is laid it starts to lose moisture through its shell, and over time this moisture is replaced by air, which makes the air sack in the egg larger and the egg less dense. So, the older the egg, the higher it will float in water. At the same time, proteins in the egg white break up, or 'denature', producing hydrogen sulphide, which has the smell we associate with bad eggs. This gas also makes the egg lighter and so a bad egg will tend to float.

Why does a cold, fizzy drink make your eyes water?

Let's take the bubbles first. There are tubes in your head called sinuses. These are what get blocked up when you have a cold and your eyes start to run. Any irritation of these can make your eyes water and that is what the bubbles are doing. But carbon dioxide – which is what the bubbles are made of – is mildly acidic and dissolves in the water to form carbonic acid. It could be that this acid, which is carried up from the bottle and into your mouth, is also making your eyes run. Also, if the drink is very cold, it will make the blood vessels in your head constrict, which means they become a lot narrower and it is harder for the blood to get through them. To compensate for that, there is a bounce-back effect to ensure your brain stays at an even temperature and the blood vessels suddenly open again. That can also make your eyes water and give you a sharp headache for a couple of minutes.

What's the gas in a pint of lager? And why does it come from the bottom?

The bubbles are carbon dioxide, which was dissolved in the drink and is released when it is poured. The gas bubbles form more easily on slightly rough places, so the points from which the gas bubbles rise are where the surface of your glass is not quite so smooth. This is a trick known by the makers of beer glasses, which is why you sometimes get glasses with pictures etched on the bottom – it's so that bubbles form there and help the foamy head of the beer to last longer. In Germany, they go one better and put rice grains in the bottom of the glass so that more bubbles form. The rate at which the bubbles form slows down as more carbon dioxide is taken from the drink, and after a while bubbles will no longer form, as all the carbon dioxide has been released – that's when your drink goes flat.

If you drop a can of beer and then open it, it explodes. So why is it OK if you leave it a couple of hours?

All fizzy drinks have a gas, usually carbon dioxide, dissolved in them to make them fizzy, but not all of this gas stays dissolved – some of it escapes into the tiny space between the drink and the top of the can, and that can happen when you shake the can. This increases the pressure in the can so that when you open it all the gas bubbles trapped in the liquid suddenly rush to the top, bringing the drink with them and making the can overflow. But if you let the shaken can stand, after a while the escaped gases will once again return to the drink and the explosion when you open the can doesn't happen.

Why do ice cubes crack apart when you put them in water?

On the surface of an ice cube are lots of little grooves and scratches. When you put one in water, the water runs into these grooves and immediately freezes. When water freezes it expands and increases the size of the groove. More water can therefore run in, and the process is repeated until the ice cube finally gives in and cracks open.

How much cheese would you have to eat before you got nightmares?

It is true that cheese can give you nightmares and certainly milk, cheese and other dairy products tend to increase the frequency and length of dreaming. This is due to a link between a brain chemical called serotonin, which plays a role in dream sleep, and the high level of an amino acid that is found in dairy products. However, it is not possible to say exactly how much cheese you would need to eat before getting nightmares. This depends on many factors – for example, what kind of cheese, what time you eat it, what else you have eaten, how much cheese you usually eat, and what's on your mind when going to sleep.

Does eating fish make you clever?

Yes, it might. The brain is very rich in decosahexaenoic acid (DHA), which is a fatty acid which the body produces, but not very efficiently. The best source for DHA is through what you eat. It is found in meat and eggs, and in particularly high levels in fish. Oily fish, like mackerel, sardines, herring and tuna, are very high in DHA, whereas white fish, like cod, plaice and monkfish, only have high levels of DHA in their livers. It has been found that DHA improves eyesight and blood circulation and alleviates rheumatoid arthritis. There has also been evidence to suggest that it increases learning ability and visual awareness. Rats fed on DHA-rich diets learn to escape from mazes faster than those deprived of it.

Why does some food cook better in a microwave than others?

It's true that potatoes and cabbage cook in less than ten minutes in a 750W microwave, while carrots seem to take forever. It's all down to the amount of water in whatever you are trying to cook. Microwave ovens heat food by exciting the water molecules in the food, and that extra energy appears as heat. Cabbages and potatoes have a high water content and therefore heat up more quickly than other foods with a lower water content.

Why does ice stick to the skin?

It's because your skin is warm. As the ice touches your skin, the surface of the ice will melt. However, the rest of the ice quickly cools your skin and the melted water turns back into ice. Unfortunately, your skin also freezes onto the ice and so the ice sticks to you. A good trick that uses the same principle is to put an ice cube in a glass of water and ask someone to remove the ice cube with a piece of cotton without getting their fingers wet. Obviously this is pretty tricky. However, it is possible if you use some salt to melt the ice cube a little. Place the piece of cotton over the ice cube and then tip some salt over it. Wait a minute or so for the ice to melt and then refreeze and after a minute or so you should be able to lift the ice cube out of the glass. (Make sure that you don't use too much salt or it won't refreeze.) The only way to prevent ice sticking to skin is to keep your skin as cold as the ice. This means that the ice will not have been able to melt and refreeze, therefore sticking to your skin.

Why is red meat red and white meat white?

Meat is animal muscle, and comes in two types which are usually referred to as red meat – which includes beef, venison and rabbits – and white meat such as chicken breasts, turkey and pork. Whether animal muscle becomes red meat or white depends on what job the muscle performed in the first place. If the muscle was in regular use, such as for walking or flying, then it contains a lot of myoglobin, which stores oxygen to help provide the energy for movement, and myoglobin is red in colour. So muscles which are used often and regularly give you red meat. But in an animal where the muscles are used for quick bursts of energy, but not over long periods of time, the muscles are richer in glycogen, which is pale; that gives you white meat. It explains why turkey breasts are white – not much long-term energy needed there – but turkey legs can be dark meat because of the use of the legs over a long period of time.

Why is sugar sweet and not sour like salt?

There is no way to measure sweetness without tasting, but there does seem to be some link between chemical structure and sweetness. Most sweet compounds seem to form hydrogen bonds with a protein in the taste buds, and that is what gives us a sweet sensation. In the case of salt, a different reaction takes place and that is how we tell the two apart. However, you have to take smell into account when talking about taste. The nose is 1,000 times more sensitive to flavour than the taste buds on our tongue.

In order for the taste buds to work, they need to be wetted by saliva. Without saliva, they won't work. In contrast, the smelling cells in our nose directly interact with molecules in the odour of the food we eat. Over 10,000 different odours can be detected by the nose, whereas there are only four types of taste bud, which are sweet, salty, bitter and sour. Taste sensations are created out of various combinations of these four basic tastes, as well as the smell. It depends on the individual, and on the food being tasted, what percentage of the taste actually comes from receptors in the nose, and how much from the taste buds. Remember how you can't taste food when you've got a cold? It's not your taste buds that have gone wrong, it's your nose that's blocked.

If you fill a row of bottles with different amounts of water, you can make musical notes by hitting them or blowing over them. But why do the notes sound different?

This is to do with how the sound is produced. Sound is produced by vibration and it could be air particles vibrating, or particles in a guitar string, or even particles in a glass milk bottle. Particles in different things vibrate at different rates. Solid things conduct vibrations more easily than liquid things or gaseous things. Put a watch that ticks on a bench and you probably won't be able to hear it through the air. Now, find a pencil and put one end to the watch and the other end to your ear, and you should be able to hear the watch quite clearly. So solid things transmit sounds better than liquid or gaseous things.

What does that mean for the bottle? When you blow across the top of the bottle, what you get is air molecules moving back and forth inside the bottle. The note you get depends on the amount of air that can move – the more air, the deeper the note. When you tap the bottle, the sound you get depends on the way the particles in the glass vibrate. Only the particles above the level of the water can vibrate, so that determines the note. And because the glass particles vibrate differently to the air particles in the same bottle, you get a different sound.

Why does microwaved coffee suddenly boil when you put a spoon in it?

This usually happens if the coffee has been overheated, or is very milky. Microwaves only penetrate a few centimetres into whatever they are heating, so it is possible for the coffee to heat in layers. If you heated it in a saucepan on a stove, the heat would spread evenly throughout the coffee as it warmed, but in a microwave this doesn't happen. In microwaved coffee, the layers are heated to different temperatures and so plunging a spoon into it will mix these layers very suddenly, causing the cooler ones to suddenly boil. The milkier the coffee, the more stable the resulting foam and the more spectacular the effect. This can be dangerous. Many people have sustained serious burns from scalding hot coffee suddenly erupting onto their face or hands. So always mix any liquid you heat in a microwave very carefully before serving it.

When you hold a cup of coffee with a drop of milk in the centre and then turn round, the drop of milk stays still and the coffee moves around it. Why?

Unless you physically take hold of something and move it, objects tend to stay where they are. The same is true of the cup of coffee. You are moving the cup, not the coffee inside, so the coffee tends to stay still. This effect is called 'inertia'. The coffee has an inertia that keeps it still as the cup moves around it. There is a certain amount of friction between the cup and the liquid, so the coffee will get pulled around a little bit, but not much. Things with more friction, for example the soil in a wheelbarrow, won't have as much inertia. If you move the wheelbarrow the soil will follow as the friction between the soil and barrow is great enough to pull both along.

Why does coffee make some people sleepy and keep other people awake?

It's true that some people who drink coffee find that they take longer to get to sleep, while others have no such problems. It's possible that the sleepiness you feel after drinking coffee in the evening is more to do with the meal you've eaten than the coffee itself. It is well established that blood flow is diverted from the brain to the stomach to aid in digestion and the usual result of this reduced blood supply to the brain would be a bit of drowsiness. Caffeine, however, is a weak stimulant which acts on the central nervous system and the cerebral cortex, which is the outer layer of the brain, and can produce a rapid flow of thoughts. It also increases heart rate. All these things help to keep you awake.

Does a hot drink give you more energy than a cold drink?

In theory, yes. One kilogram of water absorbs about 4,200 Joules (which is 1 kilocalorie) for every increase of $1°C$ in temperature. However, if you raise your body temperature above its normal level, the body uses energy in an attempt to lower it to normal. If your body was below its normal temperature (because you had become very cold) then a hot drink will go some way to warming you up. Since the drink partly does the work of warming you up, less energy has to leave the body. So, in effect, it has given you more energy.

Which will cool quicker – a black beaker or a shiny beaker?

All objects emit heat, but some better than others. The ones that emit heat well are also those that absorb heat well. If they didn't emit as much heat as they absorbed, they would just get hotter and hotter until they melted. Black objects absorb heat very well and so also emit heat very well. So a black beaker would cool down much faster than a shiny beaker. However, if you wanted to warm something up in the sun, then the black beaker would warm more quickly.

If you put a cup of water and a cup of maple syrup in the microwave for the same length of time, why does the maple syrup get hotter?

You first of all need to do an experiment to check that this is true. Put a jug with a measured amount of water in the microwave and heat it for one minute. Then remove it and measure its temperature. Heat it for one more minute and measure its temperature again. Do this with exactly the same amount of the maple syrup, in the same container, in the same position in the oven. Don't put them both in the oven together. This should tell you rates at which the two liquids heat up. If the maple syrup is the winner, it could be for several reasons.

Some materials need more energy to get a 1°C rise in temperature than others. If maple syrup has a lower heat capacity than water, then it will heat up faster as it would need less energy to raise the temperature by 1°C. Another factor is the 'radiation density' of the material. A microwave works by emitting high energy waves inside the microwave oven. These waves bounce off the walls and hit the food, losing energy to the food by friction. This energy becomes heat. The remainder of the waves bounce around until their energy is completely lost. How much energy a particular food absorbs varies.

Water is pretty absorbent of microwaves, but not amazingly so. If maple syrup was much more absorbent then it would absorb more energy from the microwaves in a shorter time and so heat up quicker than the water. Also, maple syrup has a lower vapour pressure and boils at a much higher temperature, so whereas water cannot be heated beyond 100°C, maple syrup could probably be heated to around 200°C and so is able to get hotter than the water.

Why do you have to heat brandy before you put it on your pudding to light?

Brandy is flammable because it contains 35–60 per cent alcohol, depending on how strong it is. That's why it can catch fire easily. But it's not the brandy that's flammable, it's the vapour or gas

that's given off. Liquids only give off vapour as they approach their boiling point. For example, petrol boils at a low temperature, and so its vapour is given off at room temperature, and this is why you can smell it at a petrol station, and why it's so dangerous.

Brandy boils at a slightly higher temperature (about 80°C) so doesn't give off much vapour at room temperature, and this makes it difficult to light. So, to guarantee a flaming pudding, heat your brandy gently before you set fire to it, but remember not to boil it or all the alcohol will disappear and then it will never light.

Why does salt lower the freezing temperature of water?

Pure water freezes at 0°C, but when you add salt to it the freezing temperature drops depending on how much salt you've added. A 10 per cent solution freezes at −6°C; a 20 per cent solution at −16°C. When you add salt to water, the salt breaks down into sodium ions and chlorine ions, and these bond with ions in the water to produce small amounts of hydrochloric acid and sodium hydroxide (ions are molecules or atoms in which the number of electrons is not the same as the number of protons, which means they have either a positive or negative charge). This means that, in effect, you have less water than you started with. So, the rate of freezing will decrease and any ice will start to melt. This is why we spread salt on icy roads – it makes the ice melt.

In order for the freezing to continue, the temperature has to be lowered. So, adding salt to water removes some water from the freezing process and a lower temperature is required to make it freeze. Incidentally, if you do freeze salt water what you get is not a lump of frozen salt water but solid pure water, from which the additional salt is precipitated out. You can check this out by an experiment with ice cubes. Make some ice cubes using salty water. The ice cubes in a refrigerator freeze from the outside in, so most of the salt should end up on the inside of the ice cube at its centre. Try sucking the ice cube – is it salty on the outside?

How is 'non-stick' stuck onto frying pans?

First of all, the surface of the pan that is to be coated has to be quite rough. Looking at it close up, you'd probably see something like the surface of a tarmac road with lots of cracks and lines. When the non-stick is poured onto this surface it flows into the cracks and fills them. As it solidifies, it gets caught in the cracks and that's how it bonds with the surface of the pan. So, although non-stick is very smooth when it's solid, when it's a liquid it can flow and fill any cracks that are in the surface so that it gets stuck and can't be pulled off.

Non-stick is one of those amazing things that was invented by accident. Back in 1938 a chemist was trying to develop a new chemical to use in the refrigeration process. His chemical experiment was supposed to produce a new gas, but he discovered that he had instead produced a waxy substance which was very slippery. It was called polytetrafluoroethylene (PTFE) and that's how Teflon came into being.

Why is frozen milk yellow, but white when it melts?

Milk is an emulsion, and has little droplets of fat dispersed throughout the liquid. The liquid is a solution of salts, lactose and protein, as well as water. As it freezes, the fat is excluded from the emulsion and rises to the top, forming a scummy layer, which is yellow, or yellowish. This layer of fat and protein gives the frozen milk a yellow colour. The process doesn't reverse very well, so frozen milk which is thawed never looks quite the same again.

On the Move

Fat tyres to moving bikes;
sonic booms
to miles per gallon

Why do racing cars have fat tyres?

Although you'd think the friction between a tyre and a road is the all important factor in determining tyre size, of more importance is the 'maximum shear force'. This determines how soon a wheel going round a corner starts to slip and lose contact with the ground. This sets a car's turning capabilities – in other words, how well it corners. If the area of contact the tyre makes with the surface is great, the pressure is reduced, the coefficient of friction is increased, the maximum shear force increases and the car can corner safely at high speeds without skidding.

Why don't aeroplanes spin their wheels before landing to stop the wheels skidding?

When landing, an aircraft's wheels either have to spin at exactly the same speed as the aircraft or not be spinning at all, otherwise the plane can skid. In order to get the wheels spinning at exactly the speed the aircraft is moving would need a motor attached to each wheel. This would add too much weight and expense to make it worthwhile. The aircraft industry knows that skidding shortens the life of the tyres, but they've done their sums and reckon that's the cheapest way to do it.

What's the temperature of the spark in a spark plug?

A spark plug is used to ignite the vapour in a petrol engine and the resulting explosion in the cylinder is converted by the engine into energy which drives the shaft that connects to the wheels, or whatever the engine is driving. To create a spark requires a high voltage, somewhere in the region of 12,000–25,000 volts, although sometimes it can be as high as 75,000 volts. As soon as the voltage of the two electrodes in the spark plug starts to rise, the air and petrol vapour starts to ionise and eventually a current will flow between the two – this is what we see as the spark. For a very brief period, and depending on the engine, the temperature in the spark is around 600°C, but it can rise as high as 60,000°C in some cases.

How do submarines submerge and surface?

When a submarine dives, power-operated vents admit water into a ballast tank in the front a few seconds before allowing water into the tanks further back. This causes the bow to dip first and the sub to glide gracefully below the surface. Hydroplanes (small horizontal fins on the hull of the sub) aid in directing and controlling the submarine while it is underwater. At the order to resurface, compressed air is forced into the ballast tanks, forcing water out of the vessel and allowing it to rise.

How do you make an ejector seat?

When an ejector seat is deployed, the seat complete with pilot and parachute and survival pack is ejected from the aircraft by an ejection gun fixed to the back of the seat, and pointing vertically downwards. This is powerful enough to throw the seat well clear of the aircraft even if it is travelling at high speeds. A rocket is fired as the seat leaves the aircraft, and the combined force of the gun and rocket will shoot the pilot to a height of about 90m, which is high enough for the parachute to open fully even if the plane is still on the ground.

Once the seat has left the plane, a small parachute, called a drogue, attached to the top of the seat, is opened out. This slows down the seat and stops it wobbling about. Once the seat has been slowed down enough that the main parachute can be opened without it bursting, the drogue is jettisoned from the seat, at which time it pulls the main parachute out from the pilot's pack. This pulls the pilot free from the seat and provides a controlled descent.

Why do you seem to be going slowly when you look out of the passenger window of an aeroplane, when you're really going at hundreds of miles an hour?

When we judge the speed at which we are travelling, we do it by looking at how fast objects around us are passing by. We are used to doing this on the ground where trees, houses, cars, etc. are quite close to us. In the air, the ground is far away and there are no close reference points to judge our speed against. Even clouds that are around are usually too far away; but this isn't always the case, and if the plane suddenly shoots through some cloud, you can often get a very accurate idea of how fast you're going because you have a close reference point to judge your speed against.

This whole problem might be an evolutionary relic. Our brain hasn't had time to adapt to the concept of very fast flight at large distances from the ground, and so we underestimate the true speed. In time we might overcome this problem, but in the meantime, if you look at the speed of the plane's shadow on the ground, you have a more accurate reference frame for judging speed.

Why is a moving bike more stable than a stationary one?

The wheels of a moving bike act as gyroscopes. Gyroscopes are discs with an axle through the centre, and the faster these discs spin, the harder it is to twist the axle round. Similarly, when the wheels of a bike spin faster, the bike becomes harder to lean and hence more stable.

Why do you get a double boom when a space shuttle comes back to Earth?

As long as a plane travels slower than the speed of sound (roughly 760mph), the air it disturbs is free to spread out like waves on water, but as the plane goes faster than the speed of sound, known as Mach 1, a sudden increase in air pressure in front of the plane occurs, and the air molecules become squashed together. This forms a shock wave in front of the plane with high-density air in front of it and low-density air behind. When this shock wave passes over us, there is a change in the air density around us which makes our ear drums vibrate and we hear a very loud boom. Each bit of the aircraft tends to create its own sonic boom, but they happen so quickly that the sound from each boom runs into the sound from the next and you end up with one slightly longer boom. Sometimes you can hear two booms – one from the front of the plane and one from the back – especially if the plane is going up or down quickly. As the shuttle tends to fall like a stone when it re-enters the atmosphere, you can often hear two sonic booms.

How can there be water droplets on an aeroplane's window when the air out there is far below freezing?

Water can exist as a liquid below 0°C, and there are two main reasons why. Impurities in the water reduce the freezing temperature. This is why salt is put on the roads in winter to help stop ice forming. Salt can reduce the freezing temperature to as low as −13°C depending on how much salt is put down. But pure liquid water can also exist below 0°C. For water to freeze, the molecules must form the correct structure with some kind of 'seed' around which a crystal can form. You're more likely to find that in a large expanse of water, like a cup or bowl, than you are in a tiny droplet. But if there is only a very small amount of pure, clean water then it is less likely that the crystal structure will form. Liquid water drops can exist in the atmosphere at temperatures as low as −40°C.

Why is there steam coming out of the tips of an aeroplane's wing?

You see these most often during take-off and landing, over the upper surface and trailing tip of an aircraft's wing. Low-pressure air cannot hold water moisture as effectively as high-pressure air, so as the pressure falls water vapour condenses out. Remember, it is low pressure over the top of the wing and higher pressure beneath it which keeps a plane in the air, so there is always going to be a pressure difference between the air that has come over the top of the wing and the air from below. When the high-pressure air meets the low, the pressure drops and water vapour trails appear. These are most likely to be seen at lower levels where there is more moisture in the air.

How many trees do you have to plant to make up for the carbon generated by a car every year?

A car travelling 25,000 miles a year, and using a gallon of petrol every 25 miles, will use 1,000 gallons of petrol each year. Each gallon of petrol burnt in the average car releases 5–6kg of carbon dioxide. This means that 4,000–5,000kg of carbon dioxide will be generated and released into the atmosphere each year by the car.

The amount of carbon dioxide that a tree will absorb depends on the species of tree, the total surface area of the leaves on the tree, and the rate of photosynthesis. Photosynthesis is the process by which trees convert sunlight into energy, using carbon dioxide. As an example, a 100-year-old beech tree photosynthesises at a rate which means it takes in 2.3kg of carbon dioxide per hour. So over a year, the beech tree will take in 20,148kg. That means the amount taken in by the 100-year-old beech tree exceeds the amount of CO^2 produced by the car.

But you then have to consider that younger trees will take up less CO^2, and that at night, trees release about half the amount of carbon dioxide that they take in during the day. So, a 100-year-old beech tree will take in about 20,000kg a year, but it will release about 10,000kg a year. This is still about twice the amount that a car releases. So if we had a 100-year-old beech tree for every car, we'd be OK.

Why do we get fewer miles per gallon when the speed of a car increases?

As the speed of the car increases, the air resistance, or drag, also increases. This is because more air molecules need to be pushed aside by the car during each second of motion. It's the reason cars designed to travel at high speeds, like sports cars, are streamlined – to reduce air resistance. At slower speeds, air resistance isn't such a big issue. In order to make a car move faster, we need to create a force to move the mass of the car and overcome the air resistance. So, as air resistance increases, the force the engine needs to produce in order to make the car move increases. If the engine needs to create a larger force, it needs to use more energy, which means it must burn more fuel. As the speed gets higher and higher, a larger share of the energy contained in the fuel is needed in order to overcome air resistance, and that means we use more fuel.

Why do bikes take longer to stop when they're skidding?

Imagine you are on a dry road, you're cycling along at a fairly sedate speed, and you want to slow down. You apply the brakes and gradually, through friction, your wheels slow down and eventually you come to a stop. But on a wet road, if you slam on your brakes and lock the wheels so they skid, it is your tyres doing the braking and not the brakes. Your tyres aren't designed to be brakes – they haven't got enough friction. So if you try to brake using just the friction of your tyres, you'll take longer because there isn't enough friction to slow you down.

If you look at the brake blocks on a bike, the whole thing touches the edge of the wheel so there's lots of friction. Now look at the tyre when it's locked and skidding: only a small part touches the ground and that means less friction. The more friction, the better the stopping power.

What happens to a human body the faster it goes?

In theory the human body could travel at any speed, because speed is not a force. It is *acceleration* which would do the damage, and there is an upper limit which the human body can withstand. The human body with special training can withstand 10–15 g, which is 10–15 times the earth's gravitational force. Above this, the internal organs accelerate into each other and become detached. Fighter pilots and astronauts need special training and G-suits to withstand these high g-forces. At 6–7 g people start to lose consciousness, leading to death between 10 and 15 g. So a human body can withstand high velocities, providing that it is not accelerated to that velocity by an external force which is greater than 10 g.

The Really Big Questions

Gravity to mass;
atoms to quantum leaps;
absolute zero to the speed
of light

What is light made of?

Light is tricky stuff because it isn't like anything else in the world. Light is made by electrons in atoms moving around. We used to think that atoms were the smallest things there were, but now we know that atoms themselves are made up of electrons, protons and neutrons. Protons and neutrons are stuck together in the central bit of the atom, called the nucleus. Electrons whiz around the outside and as the electrons move and jump around, they emit photons. Photons are what light consists of. We can think of photons as being particles which stream out from an object and travel across space, into our eyes, from where a signal gets sent to the brain. However, light isn't really a particle – light is a wave.

I have heard that scientists are trying to make a car travel at the speed of light. Is this now possible? If not, why not?

Nobody is trying to build a car that travels at the speed of light. Even if it were possible (and we'll come to that in a minute) a light-speed car would have lots of problems.

The faster any vehicle travels, the longer it takes to stop. Aircraft, which can cruise at about 900kph, need long runways when they land so they can slow to a stop safely. If you were travelling in your light-speed car, imagine how long the runway would need to be to slow down from the speed of light (about 671 million mph). And then there is a problem with steering. Travelling at the speed of light, how long would it take to go from London to Liverpool, which is about 250 miles? Not very long. Could you move the steering wheel at all in such a short time?

In fact scientists think that it is impossible for anything (apart from the very smallest sub atomic particles) to travel at the speed of light. This is because of the 'theory of relativity', developed by

Albert Einstein. According to Einstein your car would have more and more mass, get shorter and shorter and time inside the car would appear to slow down. So I suppose if you were measuring your journey with a clock, you might not get to Liverpool as soon as you thought!

What does $E=mc^2$ mean?

This famous formula says that energy is the same kind of thing as mass, only it's expressed in a different way. It also means that energy can be turned into mass, and mass can be turned into energy. The 'E' stands for energy, the 'm' stands for mass and the 'c^2' is the speed of light multiplied by the speed of light. It's just a number, and a very big one at that – 90,000,000,000,000,000. If you want to convert mass into energy or the other way round, and you think of it as changing one currency into another, the c^2 is the exchange rate.

If I am travelling at the speed of light in my car and I turn the lights on, what will happen?

If you were inside the car you would just see the lights as normal. Looking at the car from outside, no-one would see you because you would be travelling too fast!

Does light have a mass?

Light does have mass but not when it's standing still – this is called 'rest mass'. The definition of rest mass is the mass of a particle when it is at a standstill relative to the person making a measurement. Since light is never at rest, we can say it has no rest mass. Light is energy and energy, according to Einstein's $E=mc^2$, has an equivalent mass. Light simply has no rest mass.

A bullet is fired from the barrel of a perfectly horizontal gun and at the same time a bullet is dropped from exactly the same height. Which will hit the ground first?

The answer is that both hit the ground at the same time. So what's going on? Well, horizontal motion is independent of vertical motion because the forces acting directly downwards aren't going to affect forces acting horizontally and vice versa.

Imagine you and a friend jumped out of a plane together, and while in freefall tried to push each other away. No matter how hard you push you are still going to fall at the same rate. The horizontal force, the 'pushing' force, has no effect on your downward force, the 'falling' force. When it comes to the bullets, the same force is pulling down on each one, and that is the force of gravity. The bullet fired from the gun may very well be travelling horizontally at a great speed, but that doesn't matter. Even in mid-flight the speed at which both bullets are falling is the same, because gravity doesn't change its value just because something's moving. So whatever happens, both bullets hit the ground at exactly the same time. You can test this for yourself using two objects – pens or coins are good. Drop one from the edge of a table at the same time as you flick the other object off the table top and see if they hit the ground at the same time.

If an atom is the smallest piece of an element, how can there be things inside it?

The word 'atom' comes from the Greek for 'not cut', or indivisible. It was originally thought that atoms could not be split, but now we know they can. There is a tiny core at the centre of an atom called the nucleus. It consists of particles called protons and neutrons. Protons and neutrons have about the same mass. Protons have a positive charge and neutrons have no charge. A hydrogen nucleus is just a single proton but all the other nuclei contain protons *and* neutrons. The nucleus gets bigger and heavier as we move down the list of elements, until we come to element 92 – uranium. This has 92 protons and 146 neutrons.

It would take about 2,000 electrons to weigh as much as a proton, so nearly all the mass of an atom is in the nucleus. How big are atoms? Look at 1mm on a ruler. Imagine that millimetre magnified so that it was as big as the diameter of the Earth. The atoms in the ruler would then be about 1mm across.

If light doesn't weigh anything, how can it be bent by a prism?

When white light passes through a glass prism it bends and splits into a rainbow of all the colours in the spectrum. The amount light bends depends on the atoms it collides with. If you imagine light to be a wave vibrating back and forth, then when that wave meets an atom it can wobble the atom back and forth, just as a ripple in a pond can bob a stick up and down. But light doesn't move the whole atom, it just moves the electrons around the nucleus – it pulls the cloud of electrons from side to side. The amount the electron cloud distorts depends on what is known as the polarisability of the atom. The more polarisable the atom is, the more the cloud is pulled around and the more energy is absorbed from the light. The energy the cloud of electrons takes from the light is re-emitted as the cloud swings back to its normal position around the nucleus. This re-emitted energy is light. The electron cloud effectively slows the light down as it passes by and the light is held up on its journey through the glass until the electron cloud has returned to its starting position. If the electron cloud is pulled off centre a long way then it takes a long time to return to its normal position and the light is slowed down a great deal.

Higher-frequency light has more energy so it can pull the electron cloud around more, and if it's pulling the electron cloud around more than the lower-frequency light, it will be slowed down more. So the higher-frequency light is slowed down more by the glass than the lower-frequency light, and as the light hits the prism at an angle, this makes it bend and you end up with a rainbow of colours.

What's a quantum leap?

When an atom or molecule absorbs or emits a precise amount of energy in order to change from one state to another (from one energy level to another), what has happened is that the atom has gone through a 'quantum leap'. The 'quantum' part comes from the fact that the energy released or absorbed is precise; and the 'leap' part is because we can never catch the atom or molecule in a state which is in-between the initial and final ones, so it's something happening much faster than a jump, and leap is the only word we have to describe it.

Quantum leaps are happening all the time. The red colour of neon lights is caused by the neon atoms doing quantum leaps, and the yellow colour you get when your saucepan of salty water boils over onto the gas flame is the sodium atoms doing quantum leaps. In fact, quantum leaps are seen everywhere you look. Even in your retina, the pigments in the rods and cones are doing quantum leaps when they absorb light and change their energy levels. They release the energy in electrical form along the nerves to the brain to tell you what you see, so your eyes and brain are doing quantum leaps all the time, too.

As everything is made of atoms, how can things be transparent?

You have to look at what makes things opaque to answer this. Things are made of atoms, which are joined to other atoms by bonds. These groups of atoms vibrate at a certain frequency. When light falls on them, it can interact either with the vibrating atoms, or with the electrons around the atoms. Either way, the interaction is essentially one where some of the energy of the light is absorbed. This excites the atoms, and electrons around the atoms, so that they're in a higher state of excitement, if you like. But they can't stay this excited for long, so they eventually drop down to their usual level of excitement, giving out energy as they do so. The energy they give out is light, and the colour depends on the energy.

So, the colour of an object depends on how the light that falls on it interacts with the atoms and electrons within it. Blue objects have atoms that are great at absorbing and then re-emitting blue light, and white objects are great at absorbing and reflecting all the light that falls on them. Transparent objects are simply those that don't affect the light that falls on them at all. It simply passes through the material without being reflected.

Do parallel universes exist?

We think of the universe as being a place where everything that we know about actually exists – like the stars, and planets, and galaxies. But there's a theory that says there might be other universes out there of which we have no knowledge and which we have never seen and will never make contact with. These are the parallel universes. The theory says that when an action takes place, there are many different possible outcomes. The result we observe is the one that takes place before our eyes in our own universe. All the other possibilities happen too, but in other parallel universes with which we can make no contact.

If the theory of parallel universes is true, there are some interesting spin-offs. If it is true that the universe is infinite, then it must be true that if you travel far enough and long enough, not only will you find a planet that is exactly like Earth but there will be a person exactly like you reading these very words. There will also be an infinite number of versions of you; so one of you will have just put down your coffee, another will be watching TV, another will be eating pizza … and an infinite number of you will be doing an infinite numbers of things, each of you in a parallel universe.

I should add that a lot of physicists do not believe the theory of parallel universes to be true.

Some mathematicians say there are eleven dimensions to space, some say twenty-six. What do they mean?

Mathematicians often use other 'dimensions' which don't actually have much meaning at all. They just 'exist' to allow them to do their calculations. In fact, mathematicians say that trying to relate such obscure mathematical concepts as extra dimensions to the everyday world is unhelpful, if not downright impossible.

However, there is one theory that requires the use of extra dimensions. This is the 'superstring' theory. The whole of superstring theory is really a mathematical way of describing the interactions which occur between particles. The idea is to find an underlying structure to the particles which would explain all their interactions, rather like the atomic theory provides a basis for the chemistry of all the elements.

Kaluza, a physicist who lived at the end of the nineteenth century, was one of the first people to discuss the idea of an 'undetectable' fifth dimension – one that we are not ordinarily aware of. However, when the mathematics of this theory are used to make experimental predictions they do not exactly match the results. This is the crucial test for a theory, and the only way we can really decide which the best is. However, this theory did lead to the idea that there might be such things as 'unseen' dimensions. The theory of superstrings relies on a huge number of complex mathematical techniques (which you and I will not understand) but the ultimate test is always whether the results they give match the world as we see it.

Physicists like to keep things as simple as possible, but it seems that at least ten dimensions are needed for a good match to the real world, and there are several versions of this 10D superstring theory. There is also a single eleven-dimensional model in existence which some theorists think will unite the five ten-dimensional ones, but the jury is still out on whether the string theory is the 'right' one, let alone which version is correct. If you don't get it, don't worry. Let them sort it out.

If we could travel faster than light, what would be the colour around us?

First of all, according to the laws of physics, there is no way we could ever go faster than light. Secondly, even if we could, the process of 'seeing' would not happen as we know it. We only see things because light from a light source, like the Sun, hits an object and bounces off it back towards our eyes. When these photons of light hit our eyes and we register them, we say we have 'seen' the object.

The laws of relativity state that light will always travel at the same speed, so any objects moving at the same speed as you – for example the space craft you are in – will bounce light back towards your eyes as normal, so long as the light-producing object is also in your reference frame. You will see them as you would here on Earth. However, light coming from any other reference frame will only be moving at the speed of light, and as you are moving more quickly than this, it will never catch you up. So you will never be able to see anything which is not also travelling faster than light.

Be careful though, if we start introducing the idea that we can go faster than light, we could equally introduce a theory which could *alter* the speed of light – but neither of these things is possible.

If a perfect sphere is placed in contact with a perfect plane, what is the surface area of the plane and sphere in contact?

When a sphere and a plane meet, they meet at a point. A sphere and a sphere also meet at a point. This means that you are asking what the area of a point is. The answer is 0. The point of contact has no area.

What's it like at absolute zero?

We cannot ever reach absolute zero, so I don't think we'll ever find out. At absolute zero, which is a chilly $-273.15°C$, all the molecules or atoms of a substance would stop moving, and even the electrons whizzing round the nuclei would come to a halt. It is also called the 'zero energy point' and everything becomes in a state of perfect order with all the molecules and atoms at rest in their places.

You can't get to absolute zero for the same reason you can't get to the speed of light. Both require an infinite amount of energy. However, we can get pretty close to absolute zero. On the Kelvin scale of temperature, absolute zero is 0°K. Out in the cold emptiness of the universe, it can get down to just 2.73° above absolute zero, but on Earth we've gone much further than that and the world record is one ten billionth of a degree above absolute zero. Close, but not quite there and never will be.

Strange things happen to matter when we get down to these low temperatures. Superfluids form, but they can flow without being viscous. Some materials become superconducters and offer no resistance to electricity passing through them.

If I had a long, fire-proof stick which reached from here to the Sun, as I pushed it closer to the Sun would the end nearest the Sun move at the same time as the end of the stick I'm holding?

No, it wouldn't move at exactly the same instant, and that's because every object is made up of atoms. The only reason the other end of any object will move when you push the one end of it, is because the motion energy is passed along from one atom to the next. Effectively the first bumps into the next which bumps into the next and so on down the line until they have all moved. This happens extremely quickly as the atoms are very close together. However, it does not happen instantaneously. If the object is of a normal size then this 'bumping' happens so quickly that we cannot tell it has happened. However, if the stick were long enough to reach all the way to the Sun, then the length of time it took for this 'bumping' to happen would be noticeable.

How many atoms are needed before something becomes visible?

The size of an atom is of the order 1×10^{-10}m. In other words, atoms are about 0.0000000001m in diameter. We can see things if they are the same size, or bigger than, the wavelength of light because what we call 'seeing' is basically the detection of light. If an object is smaller than the wavelength of visible light, then we can't see it as we won't be able to detect it. The length of the waves of light that we can see is about 1×10^{-7}m, or 0.0000001m.

This means that an atom is about 1,000 times smaller than the wavelength of the light that we can see. So, if you were to put 1,000 atoms in a line they would be the same length as one wavelength of visible light. However, one wavelength of visible light is still very small, and we wouldn't be able to see it with the naked eye. In fact, the smallest thing that we can see with the naked eye is about 1×10^{-4}m or 0.0001m. Before the invention of the microscope we could not see anything smaller than 0.0001m, but with the microscope we can see things that are 'microscopic'. The smallest thing that can be seen with an optical microscope is something that is about the size of a wavelength of light – in other words about 1×10^{-7}m.

So, if you used a powerful optical microscope you would be able to see 1,000 atoms, but you would not be able to tell that it was a bunch of atoms. It would look like one object. The number of atoms that you would need before you could see something with the naked eye is 1×10^{6}, or 1,000,000 (a million). Bearing this in mind, the smallest speck of dust that you can see has at least a million atoms in it and maybe more.

Why do things get bigger when you heat them?

Everything is made up of atoms, or groups of atoms, called molecules. All of these atoms move around randomly all the time. If you heat something up, the particles tend to move around faster because by heating you are giving them more energy. And if something is moving around faster, it tends to take up more space. Imagine a group of 100 people standing around on a netball court. If you tell them to get as close to one another as possible while still moving from foot to foot, they'll perhaps fill up one half of the court. Tell them to move around more and they'll have to spread out to fill half the court. This is exactly what happens with atoms and molecules inside objects and gases.

If everyone on the Earth were to run in the same direction simultaneously, would the Earth move?

Nice idea, but the answer is no. Here's how it works, and we've made lots of assumptions and approximations to come up with these figures, but you'll get the idea.

If there were 6 billion people on the Earth, and let's assume their average weight is 60kg, the force each person creates as they move their foot is given by the equation $F = ma$ (force = mass × acceleration). Let's also assume that the average acceleration is $5m/s^2$. This gives a force of 300N for each footstep. Torque is the turning force that each footstep makes. It's related to the force and the distance from the centre of the Earth, d: $T = Fd$. This gives the torque to be 1,913,400,000Nm. The angular acceleration this gives is worked out from: $a = T/mr^2$, which gives 7.87×10^{-30} for each person. Multiply this by the number of people on the Earth and you get 4.7×10^{-20} (that means move the decimal point 20 times to the left). This is such a small acceleration that there's no way it would alter the speed at which the Earth rotates.

Why does algebra matter?

You're thinking you don't go round solving quadratic equations every day of your life, so what use is all this stuff?

But, if I buy two bags of crisps, a chocolate bar and a magazine, do I have enough money left to get home on the bus and still have enough for my bus fares tomorrow? You need a bit of algebra to work that one out.

Think of algebra as a different kind of puzzle solving and you might enjoy it more. Learning about algebra is important because it allows you to try out and understand problems that you come across in everyday life. Solving a problem such as 'I've got to get to my Granny's house 5 miles away by 5 p.m., and I'm going to walk there, so what time do I need to leave home by?' is done by applying the rules of algebra. The equation that you need to use is time=distance/speed. So if I walk at 4mph and the distance is 5 miles it is going to take me 5/4 of an hour, or 75 minutes, to get there. If I don't want Granny to be angry I know that I must leave my house at 3.45 p.m.

There are many other examples that I'm sure you can think of, where the same type of thinking that is used to solve algebraic problems is used in everyday life. Of course, you could always just do algebra for fun.

Does light go on forever?

In theory, light will go on and on forever as long as it doesn't meet anything. Light is energy, and if there's nothing to absorb any of that energy then it will always be there. But there is *always* something that gets in the way, there is nowhere where there is a perfect vacuum, so there will always be something to 'drain' the energy from light.

Let's imagine a photon being emitted from the Sun. If it manages to miss all the planets and asteroids and comets (in other words all the large objects in the solar system), it may well hit a piece of dust from a comet, or an atom of hydrogen just floating around in space. Of course, some of it does get out, or we wouldn't see other stars in the sky, but where does it go? Well, it travels in a straight line until it meets something, and that thing might be someone's eye, in which case that's the end of the matter. The energy the light was carrying gets converted into an electrical signal that goes to our brain and we see the light. Or it might be an atom that the photon meets, either floating in space, or in the atmosphere of a planet, or in an object, like a rock or a table. In that case, the light interacts with the atom and some of the energy gets reflected. That's how we see things.

And finally, the most important questions

Why is a scientist called a scientist?

The word 'scientist' comes from the Latin word *scire*, which means to know, so a scientist is one who knows or learns. Before the word 'scientist' was used a couple of hundred years ago, scientists used to be called 'natural philosophers'. Philosophy is a word which comes from the Greek words for a lover of true knowledge.

But exactly what is science?

Scientists try to understand how the universe and everything in it works. Scientists usually come up with an idea of how they think something happens and then design an experiment to test if they were wrong or right. Depending on what the experiment tells them, they then change their idea a little and do another experiment. Usually scientists can't be absolutely sure that their ideas are right, even after lots of experiments, but they can say 'this is what we think is right because our experiments suggest it is'.

The study of science is based on scientists coming up with theories and then testing them. When you test a theory it is possible to prove it is false. A scientist will suggest a theory and then use it to predict the results of an experiment. If the result they predict does not happen then the theory is false. For example, if Newton had got his theory of gravity wrong and thought two masses would repel each other then he would have predicted an object dropped from the top of a building would fall upwards. If this was tested it wouldn't happen, so the theory could be said to be false.

To prove a theory is true is much more difficult. The only way it can really be true is if every single situation has been predicted and then tested. For example, for Newton's theory of gravity to be *completely* tested we would have to do an experiment with every piece of mass in the universe – which we obviously could never do. So we cannot say it is *absolutely* true. However, for any practical purpose we have tested it enough to say it is true. So, although we can prove something to be false, we can never absolutely prove it true, but we can assume it's close enough to being true for our purposes.

You can do experiments yourself. Look at something around you and think about how it works or why it happens. Think of questions such as 'why is there sometimes a frost on grass in the mornings, and sometimes there isn't?'

That's the sort of thing scientists do experiments on.

If you enjoyed this book, you may also be interested in …

If you enjoyed this book, you may also be interested in …